FLOURISH!

An Alternative to

Government

and Other Hierarchies

by

Robert Podolsky

with

Clyde Cleveland

(2nd Edition)

© 2014 by Robert Podolsky

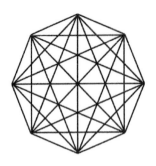

DEDICATION

I dedicate this book to the memory of my loving wife of thirty-eight years,

Leah Frankel-Podolsky,

without whose unstinting patience and support my research and writings would never have been possible.

Thank you, Gypsy!
I miss you.

— Bob Podolsky

TABLE OF CONTENTS

DEDICATION..2
TABLE OF CONTENTS.....................................3
Preface – by Clyde Cleveland.........................5
Foreword..9

PART 1 INTRODUCTION..............................10
   CHAPTER 1 - Introduction........................11
   CHAPTER 2 – My Background...................13

PART 2 THE BIG PROBLEM.........................16
   CHAPTER 3 – Institutional Analysis...........17
   CHAPTER 4 - Ethics, Law, & Government ...18
   CHAPTER 5 - The Government Robot........31
   CHAPTER 6 – Mind Control In Everyday Life.........35
   CHAPTER 7 - Debunking the Comforting Lies........36

PART 3 THE SOLUTION..............................57
   CHAPTER 8 -   The Solution – Gaia's Dream..........58
   CHAPTER 9 -   Ethical Institutions...........65
   CHAPTER 10 – HoloMats of Octologues.................66
   CHAPTER 11 - The Makeup of an Octologue.........68
   CHAPTER 12 - The HoloMat.......................70
   CHAPTER 13 - "Amplification"....................71
   CHAPTER 14 - The Evidence......................78
   CHAPTER 15 - Objections! Objections!...................80
   CHAPTER 16 - Fleshing Out the Dream.................91

PART 4 Stories for Your Right Brain......................100
   CHAPTER 17 - The Legend of Odoka..................101

CHAPTER 18 - The Real Story Of Moses And
                 The Ten Suggestions....................115
CHAPTER 19 - In Conclusion...............................147
CHAPTER 20 - The Psalm Of Truth.......................148

APPENDICES..149
APPENDIX A – The Ethical Contract....................150
APPENDIX B - The Bill of Ethics..........................153
APPENDIX C - The Titanian Code of Honor..........161
APPENDIX D – Ethical Means & Ethical Ends.......165
APPENDIX E - Why Taxation Is Slavery................178
APPENDIX F - Dr. Deming's Admonitions.............187
APPENDIX G - Further Reading And Study..........202

INDEX 211

Preface – by Clyde Cleveland

Buckminster Fuller: "You never change things by fighting the existing reality. To change something, build a new model that makes the existing model obsolete."

If you just picked up this book and are reading this preface to decide whether to continue, then I pray with all my heart, mind, and soul that the words I have set forth here inspire you as you have never been inspired before. I implore you not only to read this amazing and utterly revolutionary book, but also to immediately get involved in the **Titania Project** with all of the energy, enthusiasm, and resources you can bring to the effort.

This book is powerful beyond description. I will do my best, however, to explain just what it means to me and how profoundly it can change our entire world. This book truly presents the new model we have been looking for, to replace the bureaucratic institutions that enslave us.

Do you want:
- World peace?
- Complete prosperity for anyone who aspires to it?
- A health care SYSTEM designed to help you be healthy rather than to make the pharmaceutical industry wealthier?
- Less crime?
- Less drug abuse?
- Better education?
- A cleaner environment?
- Less discrimination?
- Safe healthy food that is not genetically altered?

Then read this book and learn how you can help create a transition to a system that will provide all of us with these glorious benefits and much, much more!

Bucky Fuller was correct that when you spend your energy and time fighting against firmly established institutions, you are going to end up demoralized, exhausted and discouraged. I know. I have spent a lifetime railing against the "system." I have approached it from every possible angle including as a Republican, Democrat, Socialist, and Libertarian. I have been a Director or Founder of several organizations designed to reform the tax system, educate people about the GMO scam, create world peace, help create the first ever Constitutional sheriff convention, etc. I have run for office twice and written two books in order to educate people about the absolute and total corruption of our government and other major institutions.

It took me too long to understand that *working through either political party is a total waste of time.* They are both controlled by the same interest groups. It took me still longer to realize that all of the divisions among us are created, promoted, exaggerated, and exacerbated by those who rule us. To divide and conquer is a very effective technique and it has been used for thousands of years to control people.

I finally realized that all of our political parties, organized religions, labor unions, banking/financial cartels, and many of our major corporations work together to protect each other and the power elite behind the scenes. The current system benefits them and they will work to keep the system just the way it is.

I have never read any book or heard anyone describe our present system and its faults as clearly as Robert Podolsky does in this book. He has spent a lifetime doing research to bring out this knowledge. Describing the present corrupt, top-down, force based system we have lived under on this planet for nearly 8,000 years is only a small part of what he does in this book. *The real meat of this book is the solution presented to create an alternative system.*

The author is absolutely correct about the importance of ethics. Without a system of ethics which becomes the agreed upon prime directive of the vast majority of our society, we are doomed. Anyone who has studied the founding of the American Republic knows that, for the most part, a very high level of ethical conduct pervaded commerce and business in the 1700's. The founders knew that without high moral and ethical standards, a freedom based, bottom up model of governance would not last long.

An ethical code is only part of the solution presented. The author also presents a model for bottom up governance that is applicable to any organization including: governments, unions, corporations, religions, non-profit organizations, or any other organization of human beings imaginable.

From the early Israelis and Anglo Saxons, who used the principle of ten family units, to the successful Iroquois tribal system; from the amazingly prosperous and entrepreneurial Gore enterprises to the success story of Visa under CEO and visionary Dee Hock; from the Deming inspired corporate model in Japan to the employee owned modern companies becoming more popular every day, the examples of bottom up, freedom based, non-coercive models of human organization abound.

The end result of all bottom-up organizational models is more freedom, more creativity, more happiness, more productivity, more harmony, and more success on all levels of human activity and behavior. It is a new age – and that new age will not come about from a policy or bill passed in the U.S. Congress. You will not change the U.S. Congress, because that entity is part of a system that is very effectively *doing its job*. Its job is not, however, to represent you or make your life better. Its job is to make those who control the system behind the scenes more powerful and wealthier than they are now. It is critical to understand that, in their minds, they will never have *enough power or wealth*.

No government or entity that is part of the existing system will save us. Do not think that the United Nations will save us – or that it is even benign. Think again. The United Nations and all its spawn were created by the power elite that control the governments of this world and the biggest and wealthiest banking and financial institutions in the world. For explanations of this fact, read "Confessions of an Economic Hit Man" by Perkins and "The Creature from Jekyll Island" by Griffin.

We must create a new system based on a new model, as Fuller says, if we want change. That model, as explained in this book, *exists now* and can be used *by us* to improve our lives in virtually every way starting *today!* As the new system grows and takes on more of the tasks that we have mistakenly delegated to top down, bureaucratic governments, corporations, religions, and unions, we will see those ancient, useless, coercive, damaging institutions simply disappear. They will vanish as useless relics of a much less evolved society.

It is absolutely up to *you* to **create this new system and make it a reality**. A new age will not happen by itself – it will be created by people like you and me. I promise you that the process will be fun, profitable and fulfilling on all levels. It is up to each of us to make this new model a reality. Our children and grandchildren's lives depend on it!!

Albert Einstein: "Everything that is really great and inspiring is created by the individual who can labor in freedom."

Clyde J. Cleveland:
Entrepreneur, ecologist, public speaker, and political historian.
Author of "Restoring the Heart of America" and "Common Sense Revisited."
Married for 43 years, with four children and seven grandchildren.

Foreword

The purpose of this book is recruitment – not literary excellence; not academic showmanship; nor philosophical discussion – just recruitment. It is intended for readers of above average intelligence who are keenly dissatisfied with the world's *status quo,* and who want to *do something* that will have a meaningful and beneficial impact on the future of humankind. I became aware of the organizational concept described herein in 1984, and have spent the years since researching it and honing my articulation of it. It is my expectation that intelligent readers will recognize, in my rationale, ideas that, on some level, they've intuited on their own – but had yet to fully grasp and utilize.

Among this group, I surmise, will be some who feel passionately about the opportunity presented herein – and who are ready to train as the leaders of a cultural revolution – a new renaissance, if *you will*. If you see yourself in this description, when you've finished reading the book, I urge you to contact me by calling me at 561-542-5800 or emailing me at cronus@titanians.org.

Bob Podolsky
July, 2013

PART 1
Introduction

CHAPTER 1
INTRODUCTION

The Shared Vision

For starters, I want to congratulate you on your decision to be a participant in the Game of Life – and especially on your awareness that human society isn't what it could be, and that the efforts of folks like us can make a real difference in the world. While you may think of yourself as "ordinary", the fact is you are not – you are *extraordinary*. I know this because for many years I searched for people with your level of awareness, and became frustrated with how unusual they are. So again, my congratulations!

My purpose in writing this book is to share with you a dream that I've held in my heart for almost thirty years – a dream that began with a question – and to recruit you as a founding member of a new *kind* of institution that I call Titania.

Did You Ever Ask Yourself...

I recognized almost 40 years ago that our species is following a highly self-destructive path – one that could easily make us as extinct as the dinosaurs. So I asked myself, "What would have to happen for humanity to *thrive* – to *flourish* – to truly overcome the serious societal problems, such as Crime, Hunger, Poverty, Violence and War that humanity has faced for THOUSANDS of years, still faces today, and will probably face in the future? ***Did you ever ask yourself this question?***

Soon after I asked this question I found a satisfying answer – which led to more questions. The answer is: For humanity to flourish, its institutions MUST consistently make ethical decisions. Simple, almost rhetorical, right? But unfortunately, most people have only an intuitive sense of what the word "ethical" means – whereas a much more exact and precise understanding is required. So obviously, a massive educational effort has to be part of the game-plan.

Thanks to my mentor, John David Garcia, I also learned how people committed to acting ethically can form organizations and institutions that are equally ethical. There is a specific formula for doing this, as I'll explain as we go along. This knowledge left me with one burning question: "How can I find enough ethical people to implement what I know?" YOU are the answer. So hang onto your hat – I'm about to amplify your dream. But first, I have to tell you a little about myself.

CHAPTER 2

My Background

The main things you need to know about me are these:

- My life is primarily driven by curiosity. At the age of five I got hold of my parents' alarm clock and took it apart because I wanted to see how it worked. (Oooops!) My folks weren't happy about this, but my father, a famous physicist (Boris **Podolsky**), understood my urge to know how the world works and encouraged me in this ever after.

- My father also taught me, at an early age, the basic principles of science and the scientific method which exist only to distinguish true information from false information. This is the reason we have science in the first place: to distinguish true information from false information. - so I became a devotee of **truth**, and remain so to this day.

- For my first career, I spent ten years doing mathematical physics and systems analysis in industry and government. Then I spent twenty-five years doing psychotherapy in private practice.

My father was Boris Podolsky, the physicist who achieved considerable notice for his 1935 work with Albert Einstein on what came to be known as the "EPR Paradox".

The resulting paper was entitled, *"Can Quantum-Mechanical Description of Physical Reality be Considered Complete?"* We now refer to it as Quantum Entanglement.

Boris Podolsky

Of Boris, Einstein once said, "Podolsky goes directly to the heart of the problem". Boris was also a brilliant teacher. So I was very early-on introduced to the scientific method, logic, and the operational point of view, the philosophical cornerstones of science.

As a student I followed in my father's footsteps by studying math and physics in high school, Williams College, the University of Cincinnati, Xavier University, the University of Hawaii (where I received a National Science Foundation Fellowship for research in quantum electrodynamics), and Harvard. I have a Master's degree in theoretical physics,

Overlapping my formal education, and subsequently, I worked in industry (Avco, GE, Bendix) and in the Civil Service (USAF Avionics Lab and Coast Guard HQ) performing mathematical modeling of complex physical systems, such as atomic reactors, guided missiles, electron microscope lenses, external combustion engines, and the like.

After ten years of this work, I tired of the "Dilbert" lifestyle and its bureaucratic environment; so I got trained in various methods and techniques of psychotherapy and operated a private practice in this field for some twenty-five years. During this period, some of my clients were business-people; so I studied business systems and entrepreneurship and consulted in this field. I used my experience in systems analysis together with psychology to enhance the effectiveness of my clients.

John David Garcia

In 1984 I met John David Garcia, the brilliant author of *"Creative Transformation"* and remained friends with him until his death in 2001. Under John David's tutelage I came to understand and value the field of **ethics** that I had scorned as a young man. I have since seen it as the most important field that anyone can master; because, through the lens of ethics, one can make vastly better decisions than one can by any other means.

By 1992 I had begun writing articles, and subsequently books, about ethics, law, and government. My research in the intervening years showed me unequivocally that the institutions that we usually look to, to solve societal problems, were actually the cause of all the major problems that our species faces. After the work I had done analyzing physical systems, the analysis of societal systems turned out to be a very simple matter. The three big offenders in this respect turn out to be **B**ig Business, especially **B**ig **B**anking Business, **O**rganized **R**eligion, and **G**overnment. Borrowing an idea from Star Trek, I have coined the phrase B.O.R.G when referencing these three institutions collectively. To date I've written seven books about the B.O.R.G. problem and what can be done about it. Four are available on Amazon.

Finally - Some Answers

So here's the long and the short of it: Humanity is facing a huge problem. A solution exists. Hoo-hah! The rest of this book is devoted to filling in the details concerning the problem and the solution.

To better understand our current situation, let's examine the BIG PROBLEM through the lens of scientific systems analysis.

PART 2
The Big Problem

CHAPTER 3
Institutional Analysis of The Big Problem:

As I started looking for answers, I began applying a variety of intellectual tools, namely:

- The scientific method,
- The operational point of view,
- Formal systems analysis,
- Archeology,
- Characterology,
- Economics,
- History,
- The scientific method,
- Formal systems analysis,
- Characterology,

- Logic,
- Math,
- Neurolinguistics,
- Organizational Development
- Political science,
- Psychology,
- Sociology.
- Organizational Development
- Archeology,
- Economics,

It wasn't long before I realized that societal institutions are pretty easy to analyze given the right tools. The first important realization that came my way was that these problems…

- Bureaucracy
- Corruption
- Crime
- Drug Addiction
- Exploitation

- Genocide
- Hunger
- Ignorance
- Poverty
- Pollution

- Race-Hatred
- Slavery
- Terrorism
- Violence
- War

…are not actually separate problems at all – but merely symptoms of one BIG PROBLEM that stems from the propensity of our institutions to make unethical decisions. When we eliminate this problem, the symptoms will all but evaporate. So where do we start? Let's start by acquiring a deeper understanding of the relationships between Ethics, Law, and Government. To do this we need first to understand the ethics.

CHAPTER 4

Ethics, Law, and Government

The Ethics

As most people are aware, ethics are the means by which we decide what actions are permissible and what actions are not. What is less known is the fact that every ethic consists of two parts:

1. A value that defines what it is that we want more of in our lives, or what we wish to maximize, and

2. A belief, or system of beliefs, that describes what actions we are to take to obtain more of the value that we seek.

Still less often recognized is the fact that an ethic may be valid or invalid. Valid ethics produce the **desired** results – an increase in the values sought. Invalid ethics produce the opposite effect – a **lessening** of that which is sought or desired.

As an example, consider the ethic adopted by our country's founders. The value they wished to maximize was freedom for the country's people (or at least for white male property owners). The belief system was based on the principles of a democratic republic honoring majority rule. What has been the outcome? Each year but two (1865 and 1920 / Emancipation and Suffrage) we have had less freedom than the year before.

Today, through the proliferation of ever more restrictive laws, almost every aspect of our lives is regulated or controlled by our federal, state, county, or municipal governments. Without government permission we cannot own property, drive a car, board a plane, alter our home, open a bank account, operate a business, ingest prescribed medication, carry a firearm, or do any of a thousand other things that our forefathers and foremothers would have considered to be our unalienable rights.

In short, we see that the founders of our country chose to adopt an ethic that is *invalid* – because its adoption produced the *opposite effect* of that desired. This does not mean I do not respect the founding fathers for the great accomplishment, at great personal sacrifice to them, for throwing off the oppressive shackles they faced at that time. From a scientific perspective, they didn't get the experiment exactly correct. Had they, we wouldn't be having this conversation right now.

Another striking example is the history of the Soviet Union, which was based on the value of material well-being for everyone. The prevailing belief system was the doctrine of Communism. The result was almost universal poverty – so the ethic was invalid.

While we are on the subject of ethics, let's consider two other specific ethics that are especially relevant to an understanding of the dilemma that humanity currently faces. The first I shall refer to as the **Power Ethic**. This ethic seeks to maximize power over others in the hands of those who adopt it. The belief system that supports this ethic can be summarized by the statement, "**Might makes right**".

In other words, those who can afford to buy weaponry and to pay or coerce young men and women to use those arms in battle have the right to exercise power over others for whatever reasons they wish. This is the ethic adopted by those who invented government as-we-know-it in Sumer eight thousand years ago. This ethic is still the creed of those who run the governments of the world today.

At first it might seem that the **Power Ethic** is valid – because, indeed, those who have adopted it have succeeded in accumulating more and more power over their fellow men and women. But there are secondary consequences. Included among these are wars, terrorism, slavery, hunger, poverty, international strife, drug addiction, interpersonal violence, bureaucracy, oligarchy, environmental degradation, and all manner of crime. If the macroscopic trend continues it is more than likely that the end result will be the total annihilation of all human life on our planet – thus reducing the earth to a radioactive cinder. Like a ubiquitous parasite, those who have adopted the ***Power Ethic*** will destroy their host and themselves with it. So in the end the ***Power Ethic*** is ***not valid.***

By contrast, consider an ethic that chooses creativity and its logical equivalents as the values to be maximized. Such resources as love, awareness, objective truth, and personal evolution may be considered as logical equivalents of creativity, because whenever one of these resources is increased they are all increased, and *vice versa*. John David Garcia, the brilliant author of ***Creative Transformation,*** called this ethic the ***Evolutionary Ethic***, so I will do likewise.

We might note at this point that all prosperity, and ultimately all happiness, derives from someone's creativity. The belief system that empowers this ethic begins with the notion that an act is good if it increases creativity or any of its logical equivalents for at least one person without limiting or diminishing creativity for anyone. From this definition a broad range of principles can be derived by simple logic.

This ethic, it turns out, ***is valid.*** Curiously, the adoption of this ethic generally maximizes prosperity and happiness, even though these are not logical equivalents of creativity. In fact, ethics based on the maximization of prosperity or happiness is not valid – producing poverty and unhappiness instead. From this point on I shall use the terms ethical and unethical in reference to this ethic specifically.

There are several other valid ethics which I choose not to discuss in this book – except to note that each of them proves, upon close examination, to be logical equivalents of the ***Evolutionary Ethic*** in that they call for the same behavioral decisions when deciding between alternate courses of action.

From the foregoing we can see that humanity's BIG PROBLEM is the fact that the world's governments, without exception, have chosen the Power Ethic as their *de facto* basis rather than the Evolutionary Ethic or one of its logical equivalents. The BIG QUES-

TION that humanity faces today is whether this choice is irreversible – and if not, what we must do to avoid the doom that the Power Ethic is leading us toward.

About The Law

In an ethical society freedom is limited by ethical law. Those who wish to behave in a parasitic or predatory manner are forbidden to do so. The mistake of our founding fathers was to maximize freedom in such a way that the most predatory, parasitic, and generally unethical persons were permitted to dictate the law, thereby making the rules that allowed the ultra-wealthy to dominate the rest of us. We must reverse this trend if humanity is to survive, let alone thrive. To achieve this end we must understand the nature of ethical law and refute the validity of unethical law. To aid in clarifying this distinction, I shall refer to unethical laws as government edicts, or simply as edicts.

In making this distinction let's ask the question: What is law? Does a person who has the resources to exercise power over others have the right to do so? If so, might makes right, and anyone who can afford to buy weapons and persuade others to use them to enforce their will has a right to so. This is the premise upon which all of today's governments are founded. This has been the true basis of law throughout the world for at least eight thousand years, since government was invented in Sumer.

When we reject the validity of this definition, as indeed we should, what is the alternative? To answer this question properly, we note first that all law presumes the use of force or power over others. But it takes only a simple exercise of logic to see that the exercise of power over others is only ethical in self defense against someone who has initiated or threatened the use of force for their own purposes. Therefore ethical laws are only those that provide defense against such unethical acts.

Since everyone has the right to defend themselves against the use of violence, it follows that everyone has the right to delegate to others their authority to defend themselves. From this we conclude that all ethical laws embody this principle: All ethical laws, all legitimate laws, represent a contract under which a group of individuals, each having the right of self defense, agrees to enforce a mutual defense pact. ***Ethical law can exist for this purpose alone.***

Furthermore, we note that all existing laws, and edicts, forbid some act or permit the act only when a tax is paid to the government. Thus, laws and edicts fall into two categories delineated by the Latin names of the categories of acts which they forbid:

1. ***Mala in se*** are acts generally recognized to be evil in and of themselves. These forbidden acts include murder, rape, torture, slavery, theft, robbery, fraud, assault, and a host of related acts long ago recognized as evils by the general public. The forbidding of *mala in se* is the basis of all legitimate laws – all other laws comprising artifacts of the Power Ethic.

2. ***Mala prohibita*** are acts which are not evil in and of themselves; but which have been forbidden because someone wants to impose their will upon someone else. The vast majority of these Power Ethic edicts, forbidding *mala prohibita,* are readily recognized by one or more of three characteristics:

    a. These edicts take resources (money, for example) away from one group of individuals, who own them, and bestow them upon another group of individuals, who do not own them. While taxes, in their various forms, comprise most of these instances, government "takings" by eminent domain are another example. Confiscation of assets of unconvicted arrestees comprises still another example.

    b. These edicts forbid acts which are ethical and/or require acts which are unethical.

    c. The enactment of these edicts requires the delegation to a governing body of authority which the legislators do not possess as individuals. In other words, they permit groups of people (e.g. legislators and law enforcement officials) to commit acts which would be illegal if performed by them as individuals.

From the foregoing we can logically conclude that the actions required for the enforcement of edicts forbidding *mala prohibita* are themselves *mala in se*. From these simple considerations we can now describe how our legal system must fundamentally change, if we are ever to live in an ethical society. The following description is not *sufficient* for the creation of an ethical society, but it is *necessary*. Absent these changes, those who believe that might makes right will continue their parasitic depredations, and the other changes that are necessary (and *sufficient*) for the emergence of an ethical society will never take place.

For us to live in a just, ethical society, the law must be changed. Indeed, the legal system itself must be changed. Stated briefly, this means that we must stop enforcing laws against *mala prohibita* and delete these edicts from the law books. Let's examine more closely what such an undertaking entails. We start by reviewing the definition of an ethical act: ***An act is ethical if it increases creativity or any of its logical equivalents for at least one person, including the person acting, without limiting or diminishing the creativity of anyone.***

The following secondary principles follow logically from the definition above and are specifically relevant to the actions of government or the "state". I've included a brief explanation of those that seem to need it. For the rest, I leave the proof to the reader.

Ethical Principles

1. **Ownership is absolute:**
   The first requirement for the formation of a just society is that the public *understand* what is at stake. The basic prin-

ciples of ethics and law are simple. They can be taught to children at an early age, beginning with the concept that ***ownership is absolute***.

Ownership is not a privilege granted by government – and it may not legitimately be denied or taken away by government except under the following two special circumstances: (a) when the purpose of such confiscation is restitution, whereby property that has been stolen by force, coercion, deceit, or edict-based ploy is returned to its rightful owners or (b) when the property confiscated is used by someone to violate another's rights, as when a law enforcement person disarms a violent or threatening perpetrator. Any grade-schooler can understand this. It is why as small children we feel violated when our parents insist we *share* something that we had been told we owned.

2. **Violation of ownership is theft – and theft is unethical:**
   As a logical consequence, property taxes, estate and inheritance taxes, duties, tariffs, and sales taxes must be abolished, thus acknowledging that government holds no ownership interest in the property currently being taxed. Of course the same principle applies to all other taxes as well.

   Under our current system, all real property, i.e. real estate, is taxed by government entities, usually at the county level. Such taxes constitute a form of rent paid by the would-be owner of the property. This practice would be appropriate if government owned the property. But in reality, government owns **nothing** that it has not taken from its rightful owners by deceit, force or coercion.

3. **Ongoing theft is slavery:**
   When someone takes another's money or property by force or coercion, the theft is called robbery. When this occurs on an ongoing basis, the theft comprises an act of slavery. Thus the taxation of revenue, as in the case of income

taxes, is a case at point – it is slavery, a *malum in se*, and must be abolished for an ethical society to exist. (See Appendix D for more on this subject.)

4. **Unethical means can never achieve ethical ends.**
   This principle, though an obvious consequence of the ethics, is so widely NOT understood that I've included a detailed explanation in Appendix E.

5. **All ethical means are ethical ends in themselves.**

6. **The exercise of power over others (coercion) is unethical except in self defense.**

7. **No individual has a right to perform any unethical act.**

8. **No individual can delegate to another a right that he/she does not possess.**

9. **No group (and therefore no government agency) can ethically perform acts which would be unethical if performed by an individual.**

10. **No government has a right to perform unethical acts.**

11. **Acts of government must be ethical to be legitimate – and therefore government acts which are not ethical are not legitimate.**

12. **Only enactment of ethical laws and their enforcement are legitimate acts of government – and therefore written government mandates that allow government to steal from or enslave individuals are not legitimate laws. They are, rather, illegitimate edicts.**

13. **Government edicts constitute predatory manipulations of the public in the service of special interests.**

14. **The same reasoning applies to unethical regulations created and enforced by all government agencies.**

From the above principles we can logically conclude that (1) all legitimate laws must be ethical and that (2) it is unethical, and hence illegitimate, for government to enact predatory edicts in the name of law.

Based on the preceding principles, we can now begin to sort out the specific categories of laws that are legitimate from the illegitimate edicts. The short list is comprised of those laws that are legitimate:

1. Laws forbidding the initiation or threat of interpersonal violence.
2. Laws forbidding theft, burglary, robbery, fraud, and contractual deception.
3. Laws defining ethical contract relations.
4. Laws defining ethical judicial procedure.
5. Laws forbidding unethical acts of government.
6. Laws providing ethical non-monopolistic services on a voluntary subscription basis.
7. Laws protecting privacy.

It is tempting to say that all other laws are bogus, but it is possible that some valid forms of law may be mistakenly omitted from the above list. So to set the record straight, here is a list (probably incomplete) of some types of government edicts that are clearly illegitimate:

1. All laws permitting slavery, bondage, and involuntary servitude, be it full-time or part-time, whole-body or partial. All taxes: direct, indirect, and hidden, fall into this category.

2. All laws that would take a resource away from someone who owns it and gives it, directly or indirectly, to one who does not. Taxes, tariffs, and real estate takings are specifically included in this category, as are all government sponsored subsidies, foreign aid, charity, and "bailouts". All government activities paid for by confiscatory taxes are included, as well as "asset forfeiture" laws as applied to those accused of "crimes", but not yet convicted.

3. All laws regulating trade by imposing duties, taxes, or other fees that raise consumer prices on all goods or on specific goods selected by the regulating agency.

4. Laws mandating trade embargos or sanctions.

5. Laws that nurture parasitism at home or abroad.

6. Laws requiring the purchase of permits before the owner of a property can alter or repair an item of real property, even when the alteration has no affect on anyone else's property.

7. Laws requiring government inspection of real property that has been modified or repaired.

8. All zoning and land-use laws.

9. Laws requiring acquisition and use of a social security number or comparable identifier.

10. Laws permitting surveillance, search, and seizure without probable cause and due process. All laws permitting government access to private records without probable cause fall into this category.

11. Laws forbidding the use of strong encryption of private records and those forbidding the sale of software that pro-

vides such encryption.

12. All Laws permitting "emergency powers" permitting suspension of these legal limitations of government power.

13. All laws proposing to regulate the "professions".

14. Every kind of licensing law, including (but not limited to) drivers' licenses, business licenses, professional licenses, hunting and fishing licenses, automobile registration laws, and laws mandating various insurances, such as automotive liability insurance, unemployment insurance, and workers' compensation insurance.

15. Laws providing financial nurturance of the sick, the poor, the elderly, the unemployed, the business failure, the bankrupt bank, the collapsing foreign government, etc. These are not legitimate functions of government under any circumstances.

Our entire court system must be dismantled and replaced with a new private system, paid for by voluntary subscriptions; else judges will continue to have conflicts of interest when judging cases involving the practices of taxation and confiscation. In the meantime, defendants in tax cases must demand that judges in such cases recuse themselves, because their salaries are directly at stake in the outcome. Indirectly, all driving and permitting cases are actually tax cases where the sole purpose is for the government to extract a fee in return for a benefit.

The Origin And Nature Of Government

Historical and archeological evidence tells us that government, as we know it, was invented in Sumer (now southern Iraq) some eight thousand years ago. At that time a group of minor kings and chieftains, who had long fought one another in bloody wars, decided to form a cartel – a shared monopoly – in an industry that I call power brokerage. In brief, they delegated some of their assumed authority

and martial power to those willing to do their bid
for these privileges.

So, for instance, ***acting in accordance with the l***
military contingent would be assigned to enforce
tax collector – who would turn over the lion's share of the revenues
collected to the government cartel. The Chief Tax Collector, in turn
would delegate similar authority (along with permission to commit
violence on the populace) to a team of lesser tax collectors. This
practice gave rise very naturally to the use of hierarchy as the dominant organizational model – which has since been adopted by almost all societal institutions of any consequence.

It is unfortunate that even the most ethical organizations employ
hierarchy as their organizational structure - because, with only rare
exceptions, hierarchies easily become bureaucratized – which is to
say they eliminate, destroy, and/or avoid corrective feedback. The
heads of such organizations soon don't know what the "hands and
feet" are doing – and thus often make unethical decisions in spite
of their intentions to do otherwise.

In today's world, the people in governments are no longer the
kings and chieftains. They are, rather, the puppets of those who
control the money supply. It was just too dangerous for the real
puppet-masters to be visible to the public as holders of public office – after all, they might get assassinated. So instead today's governments do the bidding of the real kings and chieftains, the owners of the world's Central Banks – the so-called Federal Reserve
being the prime example in the United States. These very private
individuals *own* the governments and operate them as remote controlled machines. Below is a simplified description of how they operate and why the public is unable to change the system.

Why Government Can't Be "Fixed"

Much has been said about the nature of government and how it
"should" serve the interests of the "people" or the "public". Unfortunately, I can think of no government on the planet that fits this
description – and in fact I have come to the conclusion that the de-

...on itself is a mechanism intended to deceive the public, ...eby hiding the true nature of government from those to be governed.

The description below is a parable or metaphor for government as it *really* is and always has been. Those who give faith more credence than truth will take issue with it; but those who love truth, and who won't accept comforting falsehoods in the name of faith, will recognize its validity in the real world.

CHAPTER 5
The Government Robot

Origin of the Government "Robot"

Many years ago, some eight thousand to be precise – or not so precise – through the invention of the power brokerage cartel – "government" was born. And in the years that followed, the bigger businesses and organized religions adopted the very same model for their own development – and for their relationships with one another. Today, **B**ig **B**usiness (especially **B**ig **B**anks), **O**rganized **R**eligion, and **G**overnment (The B.O.R.G.), the institutions that most of us have been duped into believing exist to serve the public, are in fact the central causes of almost all societal problems.

On the Nature of Machines

The most general and accurate definition of a machine is "any device, tangible or intangible, that augments or extends one's intelligence" – where intelligence is defined as "the ability to predict or control events in one's environment." In this sense, government may be thought of as a machine designed to forever increase the power and wealth of those who own it. Today that machine incorporates modules and components in all of the world's important institutions, be they social, financial, religious, corporate, educational, charitable, legal, or military. So it is technically correct to say that government, in this broad sense of the word, has become an evil robot.

Characteristics of the Evil Robot

Like any machine, the robot of government can be characterized by its structure, its functions, and the behavioral rules that have been built into it. It is further characterized by its meta-rules – which is to say the rules about the rules. The meta-rules determine how the rules can be changed (or not), who has the authority to change them, and by what means and under what circumstances permitted changes can be made. There also exist meta-meta-rules that determine who may know about the details of the rules, what may be said about them in public, and which ones are intended to be kept secret from the public. The following section provides a concise specification of the more important characteristics of the robot we know as government.

Mission (The Robot's Prime Directive): To serve the interests of its creators – forever increasing their wealth and power over others, in accordance with the Power Ethic (might makes right).

Awareness: The robot has a high level of awareness, but lacks awareness of its own awareness, and has no conscience whatsoever. The robot's awareness includes the determinants of its internal states and can evaluate the performance of each of its internal components.

Construction: The robot is highly complex and is comprised of many hierarchically organized components and modules, including perceptors, effectors, and both internal and external communicators. It also has "thinking" components that include memory storage and recall as well as logic and math. In addition, the robot has remote components that are not obviously part of it, yet which are controlled by the robot and/or its makers. Most of its components are people. Most of its modules are organizations comprised of people.

Control: The robot is run by an operating system, the "prime directive" of which is its mission. The operating system permits no component or module thereof to interfere with its mission – nor can the prime directive be altered by means of "parts" replacement. Only a very few elite individuals are able to directly influence the robot's programming – and they are very careful about who gets invited to join their club.

Parts Replacement: Many, though not all, of the robots components and modules are replaceable. Some can only be replaced by the robot's makers and their delegates. Some can be replaced by the robot itself. Others can be replaced by the public; but only using the tools and methods built into the robot for this purpose; and only at those times that the robot is programmed to permit such replacement.

Response to "Malfunctioning" Parts:
- The robot is able to tell if one of its modules, components, or parts is performing in support of the robot's mission – or not – and, if not, it can repair itself.

- If a particular part is not critical to the robot's mission and is performing poorly or not at all, the robot will simply ignore the part.

- If a part is performing in a way that threatens to hinder the robot's mission, the robot's first response will be to isolate the part from the rest of the system (without removing it), so the hindrance becomes ineffectual.

- If the malfunctioning part continues to hinder the robot in its mission, the robot will remove the part from its system and replace it or have the public replace it.

- If the robot sees the part that has been removed as a continuing threat to its mission, it will first attempt to isolate the part from the public, so no one can re-deploy it within the robot's system.

- Failing in this, the robot will take whatever steps are required to nullify the threat – often destroying the part removed without compunction. To this end it has killed millions of people without the slightest remorse – and it will probably kill millions more.

Success of the Robot
The robot has been doing its job successfully for some eight thousand years! Although its makers are long gone, their (philosophi-

cal) heirs are still with us and the robot still serves their interests extremely well.

Since the robot is not aware of its awareness, it would be incorrect to call it a "person" and it would therefore be incorrect to call it "immoral" any more than it would be correct to call a sword immoral. Unfortunately, many of the robot's components and modules *are* people, who choose to act on the robot's behalf. *Their* behavior *can* be properly characterized as immoral.

Immoral or not, it remains to be seen whether the robot is **immortal**. If so, it can only be destroyed by its own actions – and this is a likely outcome, because the robot is *parasitic*, feeding on the public at large that is its host – while creating nothing of intrinsic value. Like most parasites, it will probably destroy its host and itself with it, since it cannot exist without those who nurture it.

I have no doubt of the truism that it is evil to nurture parasites. If you agree, then you must decide what you are willing to do to avoid nurturing this particularly destructive parasite. If no one nurtured it, it would disappear – but this is an unlikely outcome, because the lure of power over others is very seductive to those who have been dominated by others all their lives.

Make a decision. Take a stand.

CHAPTER 6
Mind Control In Everyday Life

The Matrix

In the movie, *"The Matrix"*, people experience their lives through a vast array of computer generated experiences in an effort by self aware "machines" who "harvest" the energy of human bodies in farms, and use it as an energy source for these machines to exist. In this virtual world nothing is what it seems and everything is under someone else's control. This is a great metaphor for the reality in which we live – but the real matrix isn't pumped into our heads electronically. It comes in the form of the IN-FORMATION, we receive through our senses.

> *"In religion and politics people's beliefs and convictions are in almost every case gotten at second-hand, and without examination, from authorities who have not themselves examined the questions at issue but have taken them at second-hand from other non-examiners, whose opinions about them were not worth a brass farthing."*
>
> - Mark Twain

In our society, the autocratic class uses our labor to grant themselves luxury and privilege, all the while keeping the rest of us in a bondage system that serves them – not us.

I have distilled this massive misinformation down to fourteen "Comforting Lies" that most people in our society are trained to believe. These lies are repeated by our unknowing parents, teachers, employers, clergy, and other high-credibility sources that generally have no idea that they are repeating lies.

CHAPTER 7
Debunking the Comforting Lies

So, let's debunk the comforting lies
– starting with:

1. **Whenever someone wins (benefits), someone else must lose (or Life is a Zero-Sum Game).**

    With a "benefit" defined as an increase in creativity, it is obvious that this statement is false. While win/lose transactions can and do occur, it is also true that many kinds of win/win transactions take place every day.

    As a matter of fact, one of the best ways to increase one's own creativity is to voluntarily increase someone else's creativity. For instance, if you were to explain the ideas in this book to a friend, both you and your friend would be likely to experience an increase in creativity. Certainly, neither of you could lose by it. It is always ethical to share true information about ethics; even with those whose behavior is not ethical.

2. **Good (ethical) ends can be attained by bad (unethical) means.** (See Appendix D.)

    This second comforting lie violates the **Evolutionary Ethic** by definition, so it is clearly false.

3. **Robin Hood was heroic in stealing from the rich and giving to the poor.**

    This is a good example of the attempt to attain an ethical end (succoring the poor) by unethical means (stealing). Theft of tangible (or for that matter intangible) re-sources from their rightful owner is clearly unethical.

The most pervasive variety of this ethical violation is taxation. When a government, of whatever form, coerces its subjects into paying taxes it violates the **Evolutionary Ethic** by violating Ethical Principles 3, 4, 7, 8, 9, and 10.

The common argument, that majority rule justifies taxation is wholly bogus. To see this clearly, consider the fact that government is just a group of individuals. Let's include in this group elected officials, their appointees, their employees, and even the people who voted for the electorate. All of these people are just individuals, none of whom have the "authority" or the "right" individually to tax another. Ethical Principle number 9 implies, by simple logic, that none of these individuals can delegate to the group that they comprise the authority to levy a tax.

Moreover, Principle number 10 states that valid (ethical) laws must protect people from the predatory acts of others. But when a government taxes its citizenry it *becomes* the predator, which is not only a great evil, but also, a betrayal of the trust of the people that government rightly exists to protect.

In this country (the USA) the average taxpayer gives up at least half their income to local, state, and federal governments through direct, indirect, and hidden taxes. ***This fact turns a trusting nation into a land of half-time slaves.*** The previous statement is not a metaphor – not a figure of speech – but demonstrable fact. As long as we continue to permit the practice of taxation we continue to be stuck in the MATRIX, half our life's energy stolen from us by coercive taxation. (See Appendix E.)

4. Majority rule makes the best group decisions.
   A number of facts point to the falsehood of this statement, particularly as it applies to the election of political candidates and the enactment of "laws" by legislators.

   a) As majority rule is generally applied in either of these instances the resulting costs are usually borne by the minority;

While such a "tyranny of the majority" is not as bad as that of a tyrannical dictator, it is still tyranny - and hence bad.

b) Majority rule often leads to decisions that are demonstrably illogical. Because these decisions are based on false conclusions they have unintended consequences that cause widespread harm to people.

c) Only two groups of people actually benefit from majority rule:
    (1) Those who wish to spend other people's money, and
    (2) Those who own the mainstream media and who use the media to manipulate public opinion with comforting lies, false promises, and distractions, thereby enhancing their power over others and increasing their profits. The facts that refute the lies are rarely, if ever, discussed.

d) By contrast, the almost twenty years of research performed by John David Garcia proved beyond any reasonable doubt that small groups of people, with a little training, can learn to consistently make highly ethical **unanimous** decisions, entirely foregoing majority rule.[1] Today the know-how exists to extend this methodology to large groups comprised of millions of people.

In light of these facts it is reasonable to conclude that majority rule does not make the best group decisions. In fact, it usually makes rather poor ones.

Comforting lies number 5 and 6 state:

5. Government leaders are honest, wise, and caring, and

6. Government generally acts in the best interests of the public.

---
[1] John David Garcia, *Creative Transformation*, Noetic Press, 1991.

The evidence that refutes the validity of these myths is so vast that it is amazing that anyone still believes them. Most of us have met reptiles more honest, wise, and caring than the political leaders we know. Yet millions of people are still comforted by this lie, so we need to address it here.

Oscar Ameringer said many years ago, "Politics is the gentle art of getting votes from the poor and campaign funds from the rich, by promising to protect each from the other".

Another famous commentator, economist Frederick Bastiat, explained that government is the mechanism by which everyone tries to spend everyone else's money.

Let's begin our analysis of these and similar assertions by examining some obvious facts.

a) It is an unending source of humor in this country to point out in various ways that politicians almost never keep the promises that they make to the public when they campaign for election to public office. Mark Twain was famous for such humor, as were Joe E. Brown and Groucho Marx. Night-time talk show hosts on television often joke about this widely recognized fact. Yet the lying politicians are never held accountable for their lies. They spend billions of dollars on surveys and polls to find out what the public wants to hear. Then they tell us the comforting lies that we want to hear in order to receive our votes.

They know that they are lying and have no intention of keeping their promises to the public, but there are no penalties for engaging in this practice; so they continue undaunted and unscathed.

b) For generations our government "leaders" have claimed that they possess the uncommon wisdom necessary to solve the serious problems that our society faces. In their (seeming) attempts to do so, they have passed thousands of laws and promulgated scores of thousands of regulations. In attempting to enforce these laws and regulations they have spent trillions of taxpayers' dollars.

What is more, in passing their laws and attempting to enforce them they have violated every significant provision of our Constitution and Bill of Rights. Worse still, they have violated, and continue to violate, every one of the Ethical Principles defined in this book.

Yet, in the final analysis, government has failed to solve even *one* societal problem. They don't even *claim* to have succeeded. Not one politician has gone on record to say, "Look! This problem is finally solved."

In fact the major problems have escalated dramatically over recent decades. War, violence, terrorism, poverty, hunger, drug addiction, street crime, corporate corruption – you name it – all have gotten worse and worse as the years have passed. Today the likelihood that humanity will annihilate itself with weapons of mass destruction is greater than it has ever been in the past.

It isn't even controversial to state that government has utterly failed to solve any major societal problem. The only controversy to discuss is, "*Why* has government failed to attain any of its stated objectives to help the people by solving our problems?"

There are several equally applicable answers to this question.

a) Government leaders are not honest, not wise, and not caring.

b) Government actions consistently employ unethical means in their efforts to solve problems for the public. The most obvious example is the use of taxation to raise money to succor the poor (albeit the rich are succored in this way more than the poor). The end result of this practice is that almost without exception the outcome is the opposite of that which was supposedly intended…and the public suffers more instead of less. And the final, and most important answer to the question is:

c) **Helping people by solving societal problems has never been the true objective of government.**

To explain this statement we must consider the fact that government as we know it today was invented in the country of Sumer (now southern Iraq) some eight thousand years ago. That government was an outgrowth of tribal society and primitive kingdoms that had previously existed in the region. At that time government was comprised of those individuals who had amassed enough wealth to buy weaponry and to pay and/or coerce strong young men to wield them.

Up until that time these individuals engaged in costly, and often bloody, competition with one another. This state of almost constant warfare sapped their resources and threatened the security of both their assets and their power to rule their individual domains. In this "might makes right" environment they were also frequently attacked by lesser members among their ranks who envied their wealth and power and sought to take over rulership for their own benefit.

To alleviate this problem, the leaders of these disparate and competing groups decided to form a ***shared monopoly*** of their power over their constituent subjects. To accomplish this (unethical) end they invented the hierarchic mechanism that we call "government". The method was simple.

All power over others was vested in the leaders who acted as power brokers by delegating authority to their more-favored subjects in return for their cooperation and help in keeping lesser subjects under control and collecting material resources (taxes) from those who had still less power in this hierarchic scheme.

Such a shared monopoly, whether it be a monopoly of political power, money, oil, electricity, or any other industry, is called a *cartel* in modern times. So what are the true objectives of a cartel? There are only two:

a) To maximize the profits of the members of the cartel, and

b) To stabilize and enhance the position of the cartel's members in the marketplace that they monopolize.

With these objectives in mind, let's now ask the question, "Has government succeeded or failed to meet its (true) objectives?" Has government maximized the profits of its members? And the answer is, "Yes. It certainly has done so". In this country fully one half of the wealth generated by the taxpaying public is turned over to the government to spend as it sees fit. In some more "socialized" countries, this figure runs as high as 75% or even more. When taxation was first instituted in this country it only usurped about 1% of the nation's wealth. So we see that government has been very successful in steadily increasing the profits of its owners at the expense of the public.

Has government been successful in stabilizing and enhancing its members' positions in the power-brokerage business?

Again the answer is "Yes. Indeed it has." Today all countries are run by power-brokering governments that operate on similar principles in order to achieve similar goals. So the trend that began in Sumer eight thousand years ago continues today.

The European Union is an attempt to join the government cartels of Europe into a super-cartel with the power of all its individual government cartels flowing into the hands of a much smaller group of government leaders.

The United Nations is a similar effort on the part of a much larger group of governments to create a cartel that could eventually take control of the entire world. If permitted to succeed, the UN will eventually constitute an empire, whose rulers control the day-to-day lives of every man, woman, and child on the planet.

You may ask, "Could such a thing actually happen?" And the answer is, "Yes. It is already happening." UN plans exist for a world military organization, a world bank, a world court, a world charity, and so forth. Portions of these organizations are already up and running today.

So the upshot of this awareness is that, while government has failed to meet its publicly stated objectives, it has, in fact, been very successful in achieving its true objectives of maximizing its profits and stabilizing its members" positions in the power-brokerage market. This observation and those preceding prove conclusively the falsehood of the fifth and sixth "Comforting Lies".

The seventh Comforting Lie states that:

7. Hierarchy is an ethically acceptable means of organizing.
Hierarchy is the most common form of authoritarian organizational culture. It presumes that in general each participant is both a boss and an underling – and has the authority to treat underlings unethically while enduring the unethical treatment of the boss. In such a culture the only behavioral incentive is that of avoiding punishment. This results in the tendency of each participant to take credit for his underlings' achievements while blaming them for his failings.

In this environment it is no surprise that corrective feedback is destroyed and avoided – thereby grossly diminishing the creativity of all concerned.

8. The law is the highest behavioral standard.

While lawyers and politicians often parrot this lie, it is amazing that anyone else believes it; but it is so much a part of American folklore that we must discuss it here. Let's dissect it a bit to make it more comprehensible. We all know that a law is a rule, or a set of rules, that defines permissible behavior, usually by forbidding one or more behaviors that are deemed not to be permissible by those who made the law.

We also know that every profession, be it law, medicine, social work, dentistry, accounting, or whatever, has a set of rules known as the "ethics" of the profession. This is a misnomer. These are not ethics; they are just rules that the practitioners of the profession are admonished to respect, ostensibly in the hope that if the rules are obeyed the resulting behavior will be ethical.

To explore the distinction between laws (rules) and ethics, let's consider an illustrative example. Suppose a young student asks you to teach him how to read. Would it be ethical for you to do so? The sixth ethical principle states that it is ethical to learn; so, in the absence of contradictory information, it must be ethical to teach. So, initially, your reaction to the student's request might be to say, "Yes. I'll teach you to read."

Now imagine that before you act on this decision the student reveals to you the fact that his reason for wanting to learn to read is so he can then read a book on bomb-building and subsequently build a bomb to assassinate a prominent politician.

"Aha!" you say. "Assassination is not ethical, so it would NOT be ethical to teach this student to read."

Can you think of another set of circumstances that might change your mind yet again?

Suppose you engaged the student in a discussion of ethics, and he became so interested in the subject that he promised you he would master the subject to your complete satisfaction before advancing his bomb-building project. If you believed him, if he seems sincere, and if you remember that it is always ethical to teach the ethics, you might conclude that it would indeed be ethical to teach him to read.

In "real life" we never know all the facts that pertain to an ethical decision. We gather all the information we can, apply our best ethical judgment, and decide – for better or worse. Knowing the ethics vastly improves our chances of making a good (ethical) decision – yielding an ethical outcome.

Now let's ask ourselves whether it would be possible to construct a set of rules, or laws that would definitively determine whether it is a good thing to teach a student how to read. Clearly, the rules would have to encompass **all possible circumstances** that might pertain. Since this is obviously impossible, we conclude that any set of rules we might contrive would be inadequate to the task. This is why laws often result in outcomes that are unforeseen and unethical. They are not a substitute for the ethics.

In fact, many laws are themselves unethical, because they violate the **Evolutionary Ethic** and one or more of the Ethical Principles. They forbid acts which are not unethical and *require* acts that *are* unethical. From Ethical Principle number 10 it follows logically that in a just (ethical) society we must require that all valid laws be ethical and that all unethical laws be declared invalid. By this criterion, government edicts that are not ethical are not valid laws.

Given the true purposes of government, it is hardly surprising that the vast majority of its edicts are unethical.

This brings us to the ninth and tenth Comforting Lies:

9. The Golden Rule is the highest behavioral standard.

10. Religion is the ultimate source of ethical guidance.

To the religious these lies are particularly seductive, because most religions claim their creeds and doctrines to be absolute truths handed down to humanity directly from God. The promised reward of a heavenly afterlife is especially tempting to those whose worldly lives leave much to be desired.

It is also true that many valuable ethical insights have been derived from religious teachings. The Golden Rule itself is a good example of this fact. So, why not make religion our ultimate source of ethical guidance? Why not consider the Golden Rule to be the highest behavioral standard?

To answer these questions properly we need to look back at the earliest origins of religious thinking. To the best of our knowledge, based on the archeological evidence, such thinking began with the search for objective truth about how the world works, the behavior and causes of natural phenomena, the origins of life, and the ways and means that must be observed in order to make daily life a more predictable and manageable experience.

Today we find that science is a far better guide to objective truth than religion; but in those days there was no science. So the earliest religious pronouncements were speculative statements about the personal experiences of those who spoke. They were basically saying, "This is *my* experience and this is what I think it means."

Some of these speculations, right or wrong objectively, seemed more credible than others; so organizations formed around those whose insights were the most popular. These organizations were formed hierarchically, so it was natural that they became **bureaucratized** as their influence grew.

"Bureaucracy", you must understand, is not a synonym for "organization". Bureaucracy is the systematic elimination, destruction, or avoidance of corrective feedback. As such it is highly damaging to the search for objective truth.

But early religious leaders were heedless of this fact. So the statement, "This is my experience" became, "This should be *your* experience" – and "This is what I believe" became "This is what you *should* believe".

As religious organizations grew more and more powerful, often dominating whole cultures, they often became more and more bureaucratic; so it was only a small step for "This is what you *should* believe" to become "This is what you **must** believe – or else!" This insistence on infallibility, which violates the sixth Ethical Principle, was the basis for many forms of religious persecution, including that of the Crusades, the Inquisition, the pogroms of Europe, and Hitler's Holocaust in Germany. The phenomenon persists today in the Islamic Jihad and in various other instances of genocide around the world – as we have seen recently in the Middle East, Africa and Asia.

The Golden Rule is particularly relevant to this discussion. Christians say, "Do unto others as you would have them do unto you."

Jews say, "Do not do unto others as you would not have them do unto you."

Both of these statements can be summarized by the single admonition, "Do unto others *only* as you would have them do unto you."

If everyone valued the same treatment by others the Golden Rule would be pretty good. However the question arises, "How do you want to be treated when you encounter a sadomasochist"? The phenomenon of sadomasochism is a fairly common neurosis, well known to psychologists and other mental health practitioners worldwide. It causes those so-afflicted to value the infliction of physical and/or emotional pain – either as the perpetrator or as the recipient thereof. Since there are many gradations of this problem and the causes are unconscious, many sadomasochists don't even realize that they have a problem.

So two sadomasochists might be quite happy observing the Golden Rule by inflicting pain on one another; but the rest of us wouldn't want to be treated so. Thus the universal application of the Golden Rule by *everyone* wouldn't be an altogether good thing. We must therefore conclude that religious teachings in general and the Golden Rule in particular, leave much to be desired as sources of ethical guidance and behavioral standards.

This brings us to the eleventh Comforting Lie:

11. Faith is better than truth.
To analyze this statement and its consequences, we must examine both concepts: faith and truth.

The proponents of this lie are legion, particularly among those with a religious axe to grind. Whether the subject is faith in Christ, faith in Allah, faith in government, faith in democracy, faith in communism, faith in prayer, faith in the Bible, or faith in the market, the central message is clear: above all "have faith in faith". So what is faith and why should we distrust it?

Faith, we are told, is belief without resort to evidence or proof. At one time it was an article of Christian faith that the sun revolved around the earth. Skeptics were labeled as heretic and punished severely for their doubts. Some were even burned to death for their heresy. Others were put to death for less notable doubts. In the Soviet Union millions died for questioning the infallibility of the Communist Party. In Europe millions died for questioning the infallibility of the Catholic Church.

Today in Muslim and Communist dominated countries, in African countries run by ruthless dictators, and in South American countries run by military juntas death penalties still occur frequently. Such murders are not always perpetrated by the state. Often independent groups enact them, or street mobs do, or even the victims' family members throw the fatal stones or wield the killing knives; but the state approves or condones the murders and declines to intervene.

In more "civilized" cultures today punishments for lack of faith tend to be less severe; though they still occur. Those who question the validity of unethical laws may be harassed by government authorities and subjected to invasive scrutiny. The pogroms of the McCarthy era are a relatively recent example in which legions of U.S. citizens lost their jobs and were publicly humiliated for lack of faith in the Democratic Fallacy, as demonstrated by involvement in support of the Robin Hood Fallacy.

The current "war on terrorism" seems headed in a similar direction. More mundanely, medical practitioners in the United States often lose their licenses for practices unapproved by the American Medical Association, even when those practices are effective. We recall that Louis Pasteur was almost drummed out of medicine for suggesting that microscopic bacteria were the cause of many illnesses. He was considered a heretic, unfaithful to the orthodox medical dogma of his time.

In short, faith is dangerous. It results in rigid political ideologies and religious dogmas, which are almost universally false. This fosters and supports the manipulation of the public through lies and misdirection. It demands that we accept what we are told without doubt, without question, even in the face of contradictory evidence.

This, in turn, creates fertile ground for political and religious persecution, for genocide and inquisitions, and for pogroms, crusades, and jihads. Today we are as susceptible as ever in history to the emergence of leaders like Genghis Kahn, Caesar, Hitler, Stalin, Peron, Amin, and others of their ilk. The minions of today's BORG are more subtle than these historical villains, but no less dangerous.

If we are to escape the MATRIX and combat the BORG, we must value the truth above faith and know how to tell one from the other.

While we are on this subject, let's consider the general method for telling true information from false information. The method is simple. When we believe in the truth of false information, it lowers our intelligence, which, as you probably recall is our ability to predict and control events in our environment.

For instance, if we believe the world is flat, we find we are unable to navigate between distant points on the earth's surface. By contrast, if we believe the earth is essentially spherical, we soon learn to navigate our ships and planes quite accurately. Belief in the truth of true information increases our intelligence.

As of today, science is a finely-honed tool for discriminating (objectively) true information from false information. That is its only purpose, and it is very good at accomplishing this task. This is the primary criterion for distinguishing a scientific discipline from other ways of organizing our thought processes.

When we value faith more than truth, we are at risk for subscribing to the truth of fantasies, superstitions, rigid dogmas, and false ideologies. The dissemination of such falsehoods, in the interest of the perpetuation of political power and influence, is a great and persistent evil.

It should be noted at this point that most governments benefit from the influence of organized religion. When people believe in false ideologies they are distracted from objective truth. This reduction of the public's collective intelligence makes people easier to deceive and manipulate.

The Soviet regime attempted to eliminate this problem by espousing atheism and outlawing religion. In this case the "cure" turned out to be worse than the "disease", as Communism became the state religion and many religious groups, especially Jews, were brutally persecuted.

Let's move on now to the twelfth Comforting Lie, which states:

12. The Federal Reserve System is a government operation that exists to protect the public by stabilizing the economy.

Most people have no idea what the Federal Reserve System really is, nor how adversely their daily lives are affected by it.[2] Only the barest facts about the subject are cited here, the reader being invited to verify their authenticity via the footnoted reference. Accordingly, the facts are these.

1. The Federal Reserve System is not a government operation at all. It is, rather, a privately owned banking cartel that exists only to enhance the profits and market stability of the cartel's members. It is, however, in partnership with the government cartel.

2. There are no reserves anywhere in the Fed.

---

[2] For a thorough account of the Fed, its origin, purposes, and functioning the reader is referred to ***The Creature from Jekyll Island*** by G. Edward Griffin, American Media, 2004. An excellent 75-minute lecture summarizing the book can be downloaded free at www.realityzone.com.

3. The Fed is not a system in the sense in which it was intended by the Congressional act that created it.[3] The Congressional intent was to diffuse the concentration of financial power of the biggest banks and investment firms in New York. Instead the Fed protects the financial interests of those firms and guarantees the stability of their shared monopoly.

4. The Fed does nothing to stabilize the economy. If anything it consistently damages the economy by creating more and more money out of nothing. As a result the economy has proven *less stable* than it was before the creation of the Fed.

5. A further result is the steady erosion of the buying power of the dollar which results in the appearance of rising prices. We call this phenomenon "inflation". While we are told that the Fed protects us from inflation, the fact is that the Fed is the primary *cause* of inflation.

6. About every ten years the value (buying power) of our money is cut in half by inflation. But our loss of buying power is precisely equal to the Fed's *gain* that results from its practice of printing money for the Government to spend. This is why the Government permits the Fed to create money out of nothing. Quite literally, the government steals our buying power by borrowing such fiat money from the Fed. Besides losing our buying power, we also wind up paying the interest that the government owes the Fed as a result of this bogus practice.

7. It is therefore accurate to say that inflation is a tax that permits the government to raise any amount of money it wants at any time without asking permission of the public. We and our children pay the inevitable bill.

8. Under regulation by the Fed, commercial banks were at one time permitted to only lend out to the public 90% of the de-

---

[3] The Federal Reserve Act of 1913.

posits on hand, thus ensuring that there was always at least 10% of deposits on reserve for depositors who demanded their cash.

Today the rules have changed. If your commercial bank has $100 in deposits, it is permitted to lend out $900 ***that it never received in deposits.*** The pretense is that your $100 is 10% of $1,000, so the bank may lend the difference: $900. As a result of this practice the vast majority of commercial bank loans to the public are made with money that is as unreal as that which the government spends.

So when you buy a house for $100,000 dollars, put 20% down, and take out a 30-year mortgage at 10% interest, you wind up paying over $170,000 in interest to the bank. Under these conditions the bank makes a profit of about two and one half times what the builder receives (about $70,000) for providing all the labor and materials that went into the house.

9. What is more, if you fail to make your payments, as sometimes happens; the bank gets your house. Why? Because it put up the money for the purchase, but

10. The bank didn't do this with its own money, nor even with its depositors' money. It created the money out of nothing with a few keystrokes on a computer. This cost it nothing and therefore represented no risk whatever.

11. This example of the $100,000 house is, as Ed Griffin puts it, "like a grain of sand in the Sahara". To truly understand what the Fed is doing to the public you have to multiply this effect by "every house in America, by every hotel, by every high-rise office building, by every factory, every jet airplane, every warehouse full of goods, every farm building, all the factory and farm machinery." The result is an almost unimaginable river of unearned wealth flowing into the

hands of the banking cartel. The numbers are so vast as to be incomprehensible. And all of this takes place at the expense of the taxpayers, who don't even know they are being taxed.

12. On the government side of the partnership, the government is able to tax the public in any amount at any time without even telling the public that it is being taxed. On the banking side of the partnership the commercial banks affiliated with the Fed are able to collect perpetual interest on money created out of nothing, with no risk or cost to the "lender". The entire scheme is a gigantic scam, and the public is the loser.

13. As ugly as these facts are, the problem doesn't end there. Where is all that money going? Is it accumulating somewhere?

    No. The owners of the Fed cartel have more money than they could spend in a hundred lifetimes, no matter how luxurious their lifestyles.

    When people have control of that kind of wealth they usually spend large portions of it to acquire power over others. They do this by buying up influence and control over the institutions that are the centers of influence in our daily lives. To do this they buy up politicians, political parties, radio and television networks, cable networks, publishing houses, universities, church organizations, newspapers, magazines, non-profit foundations, multinational corporations, and entire foreign governments.

So the upshot of the Fed's duplicity is that the owners of the controlling shares of the world's biggest banks, and their colleagues, who own control of similar central banks in other countries, are steadily taking control of the world. It is this group who control such institutions as the United Nations, the World

Bank, the International Monetary Fund, and the Council on Foreign Relations.

13. Time is money.
This lie supports the notion that we should all be employees – who trade their time for money at a job. It tends to keep us on the left side of Robert Kiyosaki's cashflow quadrant. People on the left side financially are generally poorer, more desperate than those on the right, and therefore easier to distract and control – a great convenience for the elite ownership class pulling the strings.

14. If we all pull together, we can fix government.
    This lie is dealt with at length in Chapter 5 of this book.

If you accept even one of the Comforting Lies as truth, you could still be caught up in "The Matrix of Lies". For a deeper understanding of the BIG PROBLEM, you'll need to understand that just because you heard the Comforting Lies from folks who didn't know they were lies, doesn't mean that the lies weren't intended to deceive. Those who created the lies knew perfectly well what they were doing, and to this day their kind profit hugely from our ignorance.

So let's Get Out of The Matrix of Lies and set humanity on a better path! To do this we have to do something that at least has a chance of working – instead of keeping on doing what doesn't work. This principle is so important – and we've been so indoctrinated, that we have to start by looking more closely at the Fourteenth Comforting Lie – the notion that government can be fixed.

When I was a youngster, I believed most of the Comforting Lies and thought government was the answer to societal problems. Later on, after I realized government plays a big hand in causing our BIG PROBLEM, I thought, for a while, that we could fix government – if only we had the right candidate, the right party in office.

Or if perhaps we could infiltrate government by getting a lot of like-minded activists elected. My disillusionment came slowly. For starters, I had to understand the true nature of government. Below we'll start with a simple explanation of ethics, apply ethics to the concept of law, and then examine government – the creator and enforcer of laws under our current system.

PART 3
The Solution

CHAPTER 8
THE SOLUTION – Gaia's Dream

The Scale of Our Common Dreams

When I interview people, as I often do, I generally "dream-build" with them, about what it would mean to have the life they've always wanted. Most respond initially with visions of houses, cars, travel, toys and *things* of all varieties. Of course they include free time with their families and other such desirable personal experiences such as recreation and stimulation of the senses.

What delights and amazes me is that so many of us also dream of "saving the world" from fascist tyranny – of creating a new social order within which we can thrive and flourish, as a species. I believe this is still possible – and, however unlikely the outcome, it would be unethical not to attempt the transformation.

Unfortunately, this latter dream will not be realized just by expanding an ethical business to some threshold size. The goal of a million members has been mentioned by some; but I think we'll need more like thirty million in the U.S. to get the job done. We just need to think BIGGER! Just having a BIG organization of ethical freedom-loving entrepreneurs won't bring about the needed transformation on its own. Thinking otherwise, you're still in The Matrix of Lies– trying to "fix" government. I see thirty million members of such a group as a necessary, but insufficient, condition for the transformation to occur. This is because we still have not addressed the problem of how to get our institutions to make consistently ethical decisions. To achieve this, we need to continue to expand our dream.

Have you ever seen a bumper sticker that said, "VISUALIZE PEACE"? Have you ever attempted doing so? It's not as easy as you might think. Here's my attempt at describing a thriving humanity.

Gaia's Dream – The Legacy We All Desire

The planet's biosphere is alive; or so say our modern experts; it's a living entity. The planet itself may be part of that entity. Together they demonstrate many of the properties of other living beings. We call the Living Earth "Gaia" after the mythical Greek Earth Goddess. But it seems to me that if the planet is alive and aware (and I tend to agree she is) she is surely aware the way a person sleeping is aware. Like the sleeper, Gaia stirs, reacts to certain stimuli, adjusts her metabolism to deal with our changes in her chemistry, and perhaps…she dreams.

In their **Midéwiwin** medicine rituals the Ojibwas say, "The circle of the earth is the head of a great drum. It moves upward with the day…booming. It moves downward with the night…booming. We are but particles of dust as we dance upon the drumhead. Some of us move upward with the day…booming. Some of us move downward with the night…booming. Only those who dream of leaping to the stars from the head of the great drum attain the grand medicine of the **Midéwiwin**"[4]. Only those who dream…

If Gaia dreams, where are those dreams? Are they in the stone beneath us; in the bones of the earth? Are they in the oceans, our "Googol-Great Grandmother"? Are they in the genes of the planet's flora and fauna? Are they holograms in the planet's magnetic field? Are they ripples in a holographic universe? Pondering these and related questions we amuse ourselves; we doze; we imagine ourselves as Gaia, somnolent and fecund. Our vision attenuates, wavers, and re-clears. We hear our heartbeat; then we hear many heartbeats; then the beat of many hearts, the sound of a great drum. Our breath becomes the tide; our aura, the Milky Way. Our vision seems unlimited in dimensions we've never seen before. Time fragments; Causality is suspended; and suddenly our bodies are everywhere at once…and nowhere too.

---

[4] This quote is taken from a *Midéwiwin* ceremonial reenactment witnessed by the author in 1950 at a camp on the Canadian border of Minnesota. It was led by the late Bernard Mason, who was an eminent scholar of Native American lore in his day.

Have you ever noticed how it feels to dream? The dream seems to take over, as if it had a life of its own. Is it obvious that the self we dream isn't the dreamer? The self we experience in a dream has been *dreamed* by someone, but by whom? I have often wondered this. At last, as I contact Gaia I know the answer: I am Gaia's dream…and so are you.

Now I have Lucid Dreams; wherein I know I am dreaming, yet continue to dream. Such is life. Such is reality. During a lucid dream we can choose reality and experience many things otherwise unavailable to us. We can peek over the event horizon. It is a highly creative state, where we have the power to forge a new reality, a better future for Gaia.

You can follow along with me now; for as I am Gaia…so are you. We dream together whether we choose to or not. Either we do it outside of consciousness, as in a conventional dream; or we can choose to do it lucidly, in full awareness. If we dream together lucidly we can raise Gaia's level of awareness to that of consciousness. And finally we can dream Gaia fully conscious and aware of her own awareness. Then we merge with God and all things are possible.

The fabric of Gaia's dreams is the fabric of all dreams, including yours and mine. To dream of a better world, a better humanity, a better social structure is to permit Gaia to dream with greater awareness. Perhaps she dreams of being awake, conscious, fully aware. What does she dream?

We know what she dreams. She dreams our reality. She dreams our deepest fears and our highest aspirations. She sees a world of possibilities and *we choose* between the reality of hope and the realities of fear, despite, and despair. Dream with me now a world of peace, harmony, and love…

In Gaia's shadow the winds of Time are stilled; Causality is unnecessary; and Einstein slumbers. We can set aside our doubts for now; we will need them later.

The year is 511 BOE (dated from adoption of the Bill Of Ethics) which corresponds to 2,511 AD by the old calendar. On "Spaceship Earth"[5] much has changed over the past five hundred years. The air and water are clean...as pure as they were 1,000 years before. The forests have expanded their boundaries. Once again the wildlife thrives in every corner of the world. All species are safe from Mankind's earlier depredations.

The population level is stable; and humanity is healthy and long-lived. A life expectancy of 200 years is typical. Soon that number will rise even higher as one by one the debilitating diseases of aging are conquered. As the human life-span expands the birth rate diminishes so that the population remains stable, in keeping with a long-term plan to which most people subscribe voluntarily.

There is no War on this planet; no hostile factions eager for one another's demise; no inter-racial, intercultural, inter-religious, international conflict that isn't settled peacefully and to mutual satisfaction. Racism, Sexism, Religionism, Nationalism, and all the other "isms" that used to foster hatred and despite are now things of the past.

The interpersonal communications know-how and the values and beliefs that make peace possible are learned in our workplaces, in our homes, in our spiritual institutions, and in our schools; and life is sweet for our children. Today the primary focus of early education is making sure that every child has a place in our society; that no one feels left out...alienated.

Because of this culture, education is at last in its ascendancy. Our education is "student-centered", existing for the benefit of the student rather than for the purposes of prospective employers or other institutional beneficiaries. No one lacks this resource and therefore human society is universally supportive of lifelong learning by all people.

---

[5] The term "spaceship earth" is borrowed from the writings of the late Buckminster Fuller, who used it to describe humanity's dependence on the planetary environment

More than half of all education takes place outside the classroom in the homes and businesses of participating members of the community. The **community** has thus become the extended family of every child. No child feels alone or unwanted for more than a few minutes and every child has loving adults to turn to for support at any time of the day or night. This fact alone has profoundly altered the course of human history.

People travel freely everywhere on the planet and off, without concern for national boundaries, which are today as transparent as state boundaries were in the United States of 500 years ago. No one is embargoed. There are no tariffs on trade. All commerce is conducted freely and without protectionist restraints.

There is no Poverty on this planet that is not self-imposed. All persons have economic opportunities sufficient to ensure their prosperity if they choose to avail themselves thereof. There is also no "financial slavery" that was once so commonly imposed on the majority by the wealthy few who owned the megalithic corporations of the early 21st century.

Today's business entities are comprised of very small groups of individuals; rarely numbering more than eight. Decisions within such groups are always made unanimously using consensus formation methods that have been taught publicly since 2012.

When a big project is embarked upon, many such "Octologues" band together contractually, to cooperate in accomplishing the project. This way it is rare that an enterprise, once mature, isn't owned and managed by those whose creativity and productivity are the source of the organization's wealth. For this reason largely, bureaucracy, that is *the systematic elimination, destruction, or avoidance of corrective feedback* within an organization, has been all but eliminated; and a host of other ills eradicated along with it.

There is little drudgery in the world. When asked, people explain that their chosen work gives meaning to their lives. It is at the same time financially rewarding and emotionally fulfilling.

Crime is almost non-existent since there is such a wide range of financial opportunity available to everyone; and everyone has better things to do with their time.

And what is more, the meaning of "crime" has changed as the meaning of "law" has evolved; and this in turn has resulted from a profound change in the *nature and function* of "government".

Today's "governments" bear little resemblance to those of five hundred years ago. Today "government" means "consensus", an activity in which almost all people participate actively and which is universally trusted as benign and supportive. Only those who seek to injure, control, or exploit others have anything to fear from government today; as government takes nothing away from the individual against their will and safeguards the rights of all people. In exchange for this extraordinary service the people of the world have taken on the responsibilities of self-determination, initiative, and enterprise which former governments have (but no longer) sought to *usurp* in order to control and exploit their own citizenry.

Seven hundred and thirty-five years ago a creative and well-meaning group of individuals dreamed of a society in which government was, "...*of the people, for the people, and by the people.*" In hopes of achieving this end they had fought a bloody revolution and won their independence from a tyrannical monarchy. Then they established a constitution and amended it with a **Bill of Rights**. The resulting societal experiment was glorious...but flawed. The tyrannical monarchy had been replaced by a tyrannical oligarchy.

So, five hundred years ago a new experiment was begun... with a **Bloodless Revolution.** Having learned many lessons from the first experiment, this one was substantially *less* flawed.

As we waken from this dream, its power and memory persist; and we realize we are living in a special era of time, an era of catalytic change. Humanity's current way of life is not sustainable. It will either lead to human extinction or to massive change in our social fabric...or both. I vote for massive positive change. To that end I dedicate my life to the **Bloodless Revolution**, which is already beginning. The foundation stones of a viable plan have already been drafted. A "mastermind group" (*á la* Napoleon Hill) is already being recruited. The past *will not be* the future.

To realize any great dream it is necessary to have a sensory-based definition of the dream's eventual outcome. In other words we have to know what we will see, hear, and experience when we have succeeded. The forgoing pages are, for me, the beginnings of such a definition. But there is one subtler criterion that I think must apply. When Gaia's Dream is truly an emerging reality, the decisions that humans make collectively, whether in small groups or large, must be generally recognizable as wiser than, and more ethical than, any decision that could be made alone by any member of that group. When this is the prevailing truth we will know that Gaia herself is a participant in the decision making process.

CHAPTER 9

The Specification of Ethical Institutions

To realize Gaia's Dream, or any similar dream, we need a lot of leverage. As Archimedes said, "Give me a place to stand and with a lever I will move the whole world." He was right. We need a big lever with a solid fulcrum and a big hand to activate the lever. **An ethical business with thirty million members will comprise the big hand on the lever!** But what of the lever itself? What is it? How do we create it?

We know at the outset that the lever has to have the ability to transform our institutions in such a way that they consistently make ethical decisions. Every group, every individual, every school, every charity, every union will need to thoroughly understand this and know how to implement it.

So what's the lever? What does it "look like"? The only answer that I've found in my forty-year quest for answers is the knowledge of how we can replace hierarchies with HoloMats of Octologues. Here's what that means.

CHAPTER 10
HoloMats of Octologues

For starters, the essential building-blocks of a plausible thriving ethical society must be non-hierarchic organizations. The **Octologue** and the **Holotropic Matrix (HoloMat)** are uniquely suited for this. The Octologue and HoloMat are organizational models that convey a number of extraordinary benefits to their participants. For instance:

- They are non-hierarchic – each participant having the same status as every other.

- Useful information flows in all directions in an Octologue and HoloMat. In a hierarchy information only flows down, while upward feedback is systematically destroyed and avoided.

- Their decisions are unanimous – thus avoiding the pitfalls of majority rule.

- Their actions are highly ethical – each participant understanding the Ethics and committing to act in accordance therewith.

- They are highly sensitive to feedback – and thus almost totally resistant to bureaucratization, corruption and hijacking (destruction from within).

- Their participants regularly engage in a communication process ("Amplification" – see below) that amplifies the creativity of the entire group.

- They can be organized to achieve any desired ethical goal or objective – as businesses, schools, charities, etc.

- When competing with hierarchic groups of similar size and having access to similar resources, an Octologue or Holo-Mat will win the competition, hands down!

- Participants enjoy working in an Octologue/HoloMat environment far more than they do in a traditional hierarchic environment.

CHAPTER 11
The Makeup of an Octologue
The Building-block of the Holotropic Matrix

John David Garcia spent twenty years researching how to maximize the creativity of a group of people working together on a joint project. After performing hundreds of experiments, he came up with an optimized model that he called an "Octet", having the following characteristics:

1. The group is comprised of eight people ± 1 – in other words 7 to 9 people, with 8 being best.

2. The group is comprised of four men and four women ± 1 – again 4x4 is best, but 3x4 or 4x5 is acceptable.

3. The group members all understand the principles of Ethics as exemplified by the **Bill of Ethics** and are committed to acting ethically to the best of their ability.

4. Participation in the group is voluntary. Anyone can quit at any time for any reason.

5. Only unanimous decisions by the group are recognized as true group decisions.

6. A group member can only be expelled by the group if all the other members agree unanimously. And of course an individual can leave the group for any reason if they wish to do so.

7. The group has been trained in a communication protocol that facilitates the making of unanimous decisions.

8. The group meets as often as it likes – once a week often being optimal – once a month being the least frequent occurrence that works – specifically to engage in a communication protocol called ""Amplification"" (described below), a process that *amplifies* the group's creativity.

9. The group need not engage in "Amplification" at every meeting; but should do so at least once a month for meaningful results.

I was friends with John David for 17 years, until he passed away in 2001: and I participated in a number of his experiments in the field of maximizing creativity. My main personal contribution to John David's work was to improve on his method of "Amplification". In John David's Octets, it took several days of training for a group of eight to learn the process. Using my knowledge of Neurolinguistic Programming (NLP) and my 20 years experience as a clinical psychotherapist, I shortened the training time to just a few hours. Also, the onset of the "Amplification" phenomenon occurs much faster with my method. I call an Octet using my model of "Amplification" an "Octologue". Details of the "Amplification" process are described below – but first let's turn to the HoloMat.

CHAPTER 12
The Holotropic Matrix – or HoloMat

It is obvious that many worthwhile projects require more than eight people. The solution is simple – the project is undertaken by multiple Octologues that have entered into an ethical contract with each other. More than twenty years ago I decided to call such a contractual concatenation of Octologues a Holotropic Matrix – or HoloMat for short – drawing a parallel between the way a hologram distributes information in such a way that the information contained is available throughout the hologram – and the way a HoloMat distributes both information and responsibility.

There is no practical limit to the size of a HoloMat. For really big projects, a HoloMat could have millions of members – or even tens of millions.

One of the biggest differences between a hierarchy and a HoloMat is that a hierarchy is designed to avoid, eliminate or destroy corrective feedback and a HoloMat is designed to elicit and encourage corrective feedback. In a Hierarchy the information flows down; in a HoloMat information flows in all directions! Any participant in the HoloMat can give corrective feedback that will be valuable and be heard in any segment of the organization! - Whereas, in a hierarchy if they wanted your opinion, they would be giving it to you!

CHAPTER 13
"Amplification" – The Most Unique Feature of Octologues and Holo-Mats

Trance: In order to explain "Amplification" most succinctly, it is necessary to explain the word "trance" – a word that is much maligned and often misunderstood. Some people fear trance, thinking it's a supernatural phenomenon – or even a "tool of the devil". This is utter nonsense! Trance is merely something *you do*. It's a label for paying attention to your sensory experience in a way that is different from what you do most of the time. It's a totally natural phenomenon. It should be noted that trance states are indistinguishable from meditative states – and as such are totally benign.

Almost everyone is in a trance at least twice a day, once when waking up from sleep or in the process of falling asleep, you go through a stage where you are neither really asleep nor awake – it's a trance state, an "altered state of conscious".

Similarly, when you are driving on a straight road with monotonous roadsides, you will often enter a "driving trance", in which you are driving competently but also thinking of other things. You usually become aware of this when you approach your destination and realize that the time that has passed while you were driving "feels" less than you know it had to be. Such time distortion is one of many things you can do in trance that you can't readily do in your normal state of awareness.

Other examples of Trances are when you are in a casino. Every sensory stimulus in the casino from the design of the floors, the organization of the tables and machines, the sounds you hear is put there to induce a trace state; so you will continue to give them your money! Ever notice how hard it is to find the door exiting the casino?

Even the grocery store layout is designed to put you in trance, from the coloring of the containers, the music playing, even the temperature is there for a reason. That reason again: to have you give them your money. Many assert that going to church, or any kind of spiritual experience, puts them into a trance as well.

Guided Meditation: While we're on the subject of trance, let's briefly talk about "guided meditation" – another phrase that is much misunderstood. When you participate in guided meditation, the operator (guide) does not "put" you in a trance; nor can you be forced into a trance (barring the use of drugs). Rather the operator *leads* you into the trance state.

Imagine I hold up my hand and *ask you* to look at it. You are, of course, free to refuse – or to do something completely different from what I've asked of you. So it is with guided meditation. The difference is that *it is your subconscious that decides how you will respond* – and in most people the subconscious is innately curious – and happy to learn new ways of perceiving. So trance is just another kind of learning experience.

"Amplification" – Finally

So what is "Amplification" and how does it work? Here are the basics. In a nutshell, "Amplification" is a group trance state (or group meditative state). The members of an Octologue sit on comfortable chairs in a tight circle with their arms on the shoulders of their neighbors. Bare feet touch in the middle of the circle. A Bach fugue plays softly in the background. A meditation facilitator leads the experience verbally, making direct and indirect suggestions that enable the members of the group to alter their consciousness in a particular manner. The rules to which the group members have agreed are simple:

- A subject of interest has been agreed upon and discussed before the session;

- Each member is encouraged to think about the subject with both his/her conscious and subconscious minds;

- When a thought occurs to a member that seems interesting, and the member feels an urge to share the thought aloud, he/she withholds the information the first time the urge to speak occurs;

- If the thought recurs, the person thinking it is obliged to speak it aloud – no matter how strange, weird, obscene, irrational, bizarre, or otherwise nonsensical it may seem.

- The session continues until someone (anyone) in the group requests that it end.

- Such sessions are usually recorded for later play-back – because participants often don't recall what has been said – even if *they* were the one to have spoken.

It should be noted that it is often the strangest comments made during Amplification that turn out to be the most creative and useful when carefully examined later. By this means the Octologue accesses information that no one in the group could access on their own – though many creative individuals use altered "mystical" states as part of their creative methodology. Still, the synergy of the group trance seems to act as an amplifier of each individual's creativity – thus yielding a level of innovation greater than the sum of the individual participants' capabilities.

What Is the "Amplification" Experience Like?

Some people appear to go to sleep – though this doesn't prevent them from speaking. For most participants, the best description of the experience is that of a "shared lucid dream". The process involves a still yet to be understood phenomenon occurring in the recesses of the subconscious, manifested as a result of group rapport.

The "Amplification" process is one of group rapport, whereby the trance state induces the maximization of creativity by amplifying humans' ability to reach out to the "great beyond" and bring back new INFORMATION! "Amplification" is pleasant; it may be exciting at times; and many feel saddened or disappointed when it is over. This description applies equally well to some other forms of meditatively induced group trances.

A small percentage of individuals are frightened by the closeness of the "Amplification" experience – and it only takes one such person in the Octologue for the "Amplification" ***not to work***. For this reason it is important that a new recruit in an Octologue be comfortable with the process before being formally included as a member of the group.

How Does It work?

We don't really know *for sure* how "Amplification" works – but we have a hypothesis that fits the facts. According to author Michael Talbot, the universe is holographic.[1] If this hypothesis is correct, and there is much evidence to support it, all the information that exists in the universe is available everywhere.

A second postulate of the hypothesis is that the human brain is a quantum mechanical "machine" that is able, under the right conditions, to reach out into the holographic *quantum* universe and retrieve whatever information it is seeking – including both true information and false information. Science provides the tools and methodology by means of which we determine whether new information is true or false.

---

[1] See ***The Holographic Universe*** by Michael Talbot, Harper Perennial, 1991.

I must also point out that the Religious Society of Friends (a.k.a. Quakers) employs a method of group decision-making that bears some striking similarities to "Amplification".[2] Quiet contemplation... awaiting the inspiration of God... distrust of initial urges to speak... obligation to speak when the "presence" is perceived... requirement of unanimity for decisions... and much more. For certain, sitting in empty silence waiting for God's presence to be felt...and God's wishes to be heard and understood constitutes an "altered state of awareness" if there ever was one. Moreover, as John David Garcia pointed out, the creative acts of every great scientist may be seen as "mystical" experiences – making each a "scientific mystic" – distinctly different from a "mystical scientist".[3]

---

[2] See: ***Beyond Majority Rule*** by Michael J. Sheeran, published in 1983 by the Philadelphia Yearly Meeting of the Religious Society of Friends.

[3] See *Creative Transformation* by John David Garcia.

The Grand Experiment
John David proved unequivocally, through hundreds of scientific experiments, that this process maximizes creativity in groups. Creativity is what has brought us fire, the renaissance, the chair you are sitting on, and the book you are reading. Yet humanity is fraught with problems.

Let us release ourselves from this self imposed bondage using our own creativity to find a way out of the mess we CREATED in the first place. I am prepared to share the knowledge of how we may be able to do this with those individuals whose personal evolution brings us together. Let's perform the "Grand Experiment" together, in LIFE, lest this be our last generation. Albert Einstein said "I know not with what weapons World War III will be fought, but World War IV will be fought with sticks and stones".

THE TRANSITION IS LIFE

- So let's recap what we've learned thus far.
  Most of us have a shared sense of destiny that includes a burning desire to change the world beneficially. This is akin to the traditional Jewish dream of "Tikkun" – the healing of the world.

- We recognize that realizing such a dream requires us to restructure our institutions in such a way that they consistently make **ethical decisions** – an impossible feat as long as our institutions remain hierarchy-based.

- We know that those who agree with the precepts in this book are decent people – folks with a pretty good intuitive sense of right and wrong (the ethics).

- We can see that for us to succeed, we have to get over thinking that any kind of government can be fixed. The game is rigged. Instead of fixing something that causes problems in the first place, we will create a new institution. One that is Ethical and Creative.

- We are confident that we can increase our numbers to the point where we can wield a "big hand" on the "move-the-world" lever. I've suggested thirty million as a potential tipping point; because 10% of a population is usually sufficient to change the course of that population's history. Though Oliver deMille suggests that 1.5 to 2 % will suffice, my experience leads me to believe a higher number is needed.

- And finally, we have a lever that is big enough and solid enough to do the job. The "lever" is just the act of teaching the world how to replace hierarchies with HoloMats of Octologues. I call this lever the **Titania Project**. To put this **lever** on its fulcrum, all we have to do is to vigorously market the Know-how contained in this book. The resulting product line includes books (already written), DVDs and CDs of presentations (yet to be given as of this writing), and three workshops that are already designed.

CHAPTER 14
THE EVIDENCE

The Evidence

The power of the Titania concept isn't just the dynamics of Octologues and HoloMats – not by far. The real power lies in the Ethics. When a group with an ethical purpose commits to making unanimous ethical decisions, the resulting outcomes are *amazing!* But of course, the logical question is, "Where is the proof?"

In APPENDIX E you will find a detailed step-by-logical-step statement of the proof. As anything worthy of the designation "proof" tends to be, it's a bit hairy in its complexity – though unchallenged in its execution and conclusions. For those not wishing to wade through the logic in detail, I provide the following overview.

In 1993 I sat down with my friend Greg Sulliger and together wrote a document called ***The Bill of Ethics*** – in which we provided the means whereby any organization wishing to constrain its actions to those that are ethical could take the first giant step in this direction by using the document to amend their constitution, charter, or bylaws. You can read this document in APPENDIX C.

It was about ten years later that I learned how Japanese industry saved itself from oblivion by adopting a set of suggestions that were provided by Dr. William Edward Deming, a successful American industrialist. In five years Japanese industry showed significant improvement. In ten years it had become highly competitive internationally. And in fifteen years it dominated almost every manufacturing market in the world.

Though Deming made no explicit mention of ethics, I recognized from his suggestions that an organization adopting his suggestions would become far more likely to make ethical decisions. So I set out to discover the logical relationship between Deming's suggestions and the requirements imposed by *The Bill of Ethics.*

To my surprise and delight, I discovered that every one of Deming's suggestions could be derived as a logical consequence of the Ethics. Think about that for a moment. It means that if Japanese industry had adopted *The Bill of Ethics* in 1950, instead of Deming's suggestions, the same wonderful transformation of Japanese industry would have occurred – at the very least. The conclusion is inescapable: THE ETHICS WORKS! Adopting the Ethics leads to success on a scale otherwise unimaginable. And that's what the **Titania Project** is all about. The strategy of using HoloMats of Octologues is merely a very good example of how one can implement the Ethics in an organization in a manner that avoids bureaucratization – permanently!

CHAPTER 15

Objections! Objections!

There are many, especially among the BORG, who will criticize the ideas that I have shared with you in these pages. So I thought it might be helpful for you to know, in advance, what some critics might say. The list that follows is an incomplete sample of the likely criticisms; but I think it is illustrative of what you may reasonably expect as you share this information with others.

1. One major category of criticisms that I am certain will arise will take the form of assertions that one or more of the Comforting Lies are, in fact, true statements. Such a criticism will usually be made indirectly; which is to say that the critic will not directly state that a particular Lie is truth; but instead will make a criticism that **presupposes** the righteousness of the Lie. If you can recognize which Lie the critic embraces you can show that the criticism **requires** belief in the Lie, and then refute the criticism by refuting the Lie.

2. A second category of criticism will take our ideas to task for failing to acknowledge the critic's favorite source of truth as the one-and-only source of truth. The source of truth preferred by the critic may be the Bible, the writings of the "founding fathers", the pronouncements of their favorite politician, the favorite sayings of a revered ancestor, or the opinions of their favorite talk-show host.

    No matter what their preference, you need to understand that this critic isn't really participating in the conversation at hand. Instead they are either seeking your ratification of their own personal prejudice or faith, or they are seeking to use your forum to promote their own dogmatic agenda. If their agenda presumes the truth of one of the Comforting Lies, you can proceed as in (1) above. If not, their agenda probably isn't particularly relevant to the conversation at hand. You can politely (or not) bring the discussion back on track. Your failure to esteem their favorite guru is not actually a criticism of these ideas. It is, rather, an irrelevancy. You would do well to treat it as such.

3. Before we go any further I should mention the critics who say that it is arrogant or presumptuous of us to suggest a way we can save humanity from itself. They say things like, "Who do you think you are to make such grandiose (ambitious) utopian (unattainable) plans?" You will doubtless meet such critics if you become a proponent of an ethical way of thinking.

   You need to understand that this class of critics is not concerned with the question of whether your plan is valid. They are, rather, afraid of the disappointment they would experience if the plan failed. They are, in effect, arguing for your acceptance of their own perceived limitations. Treat these individuals with gentle kindness; but don't turn ***their*** limitations into ***your*** limitations.

   Simply remember that every massive societal transformation (good or bad), for better or worse, began as an idea in the mind of some innovative individual. Genghis Khan, Baruch de Spinoza, Plato, Copernicus, Galileo, Marie Curie, Thomas Jefferson, Karl Marx, Louis Pasteur, Alexander the Great, Adolph Hitler, Albert Einstein, Abraham, Confucius, Muhammad, Jesus, William Deming, Martin Luther King, and Mother Teresa, to name just a few, all stood alone at one time, knowing little or nothing of what impact their ideas would have on mankind's future.

   Most of them had no special credentials to enhance their credibility, no state-conferred license to practice their art, and no vast fortunes to finance their followers' belief in their ideas. I am fortunate that I grew up in a family that supported innovation and in which it was not unheard-of for ordinary people to attain extraordinary achievements. You may not have been so fortunate; but only you can keep you from acting (taking action) ***as if you had***.

So be kind and understanding toward those whose criticism stems from their fear of failure. Many of them will follow willingly in your footsteps once you have overcome some obstacles and reduced the perceived risks inherent in your path. What seems a "bump in the road" to you may seem a potential land mine to them. So be sympathetic and persevere.

4. Two common criticisms of our plan are that "it's too liberal" or "it's too conservative". It may be perceived either way, depending upon the pet prejudices of the critic. In either case the critic obviously has not studied our plan enough to really understand it, and is also influenced by one or more of the Comforting Lies. The liberal critic often embraces the Robin Hood Lie, while the conservative critic is likely to believe in the Democratic Lie.

Critics in both camps tend to blame one another for the Big Problem rather than make the effort to analyze its actual causes. Their one-dimensional analysis is simply the only tool they have to understand the events that occur in the world around them. When the only tool you have is a hammer, every problem looks to you like a nail.

The easiest and most respectful way of which we know to respond to these critics is with a clarifying question, such as, "How, specifically, is it too liberal?" or "What makes it too conservative?" The critic's answer to either of these questions usually reveals their level of understanding of our ideas, their level of understanding of the liberal-conservative distinction, and the nature of their underlying fear or anxiety engendered by our proposals. Once you have this information you will find it much easier to respond appropriately to the critic's concern.

5. "Your plan is anarchic; it can only lead to chaos and violence" is another criticism of our plan that you will encounter. This is yet another instance of a critic's lack of understanding of what we actually propose. Yes, we suggest doing away with the institution of government. But rather than opt for chaos, we propose replacing government with a fundamentally different **kind** of institution, one whose purposes, laws, and decision-making processes are inherently more ethical and humane than those now sanctioned by the BORG.

   What is more, our plan outlines an orderly non-violent process by which we can make the transition from today's system to the future system that we envisage; so this criticism misses its mark, because it addresses some plan fantasized by the critic, and not our actual plan at all.

6. You will also hear, "If your plan is so good, why don't you make it your platform and run for office on it, thereby offering to fix government from within?" This is a valid and thoughtful criticism that should be taken seriously.

   For the success of the Titania plan it may, in fact, be **necessary** for many politically inclined individuals to run on our platform; but we doubt it will be **sufficient** for success until millions of people are already participating in Octologues and HoloMats. Until that time we believe we can contribute more and be more effective outside the system.

   You (the reader), on the other hand, may have the political resources and inclinations best suited to pursue this valuable experiment. If so, we would encourage you to do so.

Such a course of action, while insufficient for the inauguration of ethical change, may in fact be necessary.

7. Some will say our plan is "unconstitutional", "un-American", or even "illegal". This is simply not so. The Constitution for the United States of America provides a mechanism for its own evolution by the legal and peaceful means of amendment. In this the writers of the Constitution did well.

    It is unfortunate that they didn't give more thought (and more ink) to defining how a good amendment might be differentiated from a bad amendment. Adoption of the **Bill of Ethics** would provide this missing know-how.

    In the absence of this, or an equivalent, formulation, the "defenders" of the Constitution have impeded its evolution by casting it in a block of more-or-less immutable political polymer and by enshrining it in the myth of the "infallible founding fathers".

    Of course, a further massive complication is the fact that in the last ten years the relevance of the Constitution has been effectively nullified by the Patriot Act, the Military Commissions Act, and more recently the passage of the National Defense Authorization Act. So don't expect fixing the Constitution to be particularly effective.

    It is our belief that, if the writers of the Constitution had our two hundred years of 20/20 hindsight, they would have been very pleased with our proposals and would have eagerly incorporated them into our original constitution. What do you think?

8. Many critics of our plan ask questions of the form, "How would your plan solve the problem of X?" where X represents war, hunger, poverty, illicit drugs, environmental

degradation, inner-city crime, terrorism, the AIDS plague, Middle-East strife, or any other current manifestation of the Big Problem. "What's your solution?" they ask. Wow! It's really very flattering in a way. At least they are taking the plan seriously enough to ask the question. We think the critic actually hopes we have that particular problem all thought out.

Well, sad to say, we don't have all the answers…yet. Whatever problematic manifestation is your favorite, the one that riles you up, how about you apply our tools and solve it yourself as a student exercise? That is our answer to that particular flavor of challenge.

We will say this. We are confident that when enough people are working our plan, that all those manifest problems will be solved. It may take a hundred years for us to get to that point; or it might take two hundred years, or five hundred years; but we can see no reason why the plan should fail, providing we don't exterminate ourselves in the meantime.

9. "Your plan will never work", is the criticism that you are likely to hear most often. Strictly speaking, this remark is not a criticism at all. It is, rather, an assertion that the plan violates the critic's belief system in some way. Coming from that mind-set, a more sophisticated critic will sometimes ask, "What makes you think your plan will work?" Unlike some of the other critics we have discussed, this critic may actually be asking for more information. He/she is asking to be convinced or persuaded that your plan merits their conviction. It behooves you to oblige.

At this point you will find it helpful to gather a little more information concerning the critic's reservations about your plan. To do this you can simply ask, "Why not?" or "What makes you think it **won't** work?" Is the current system of hierarchic controls "working"? Listen carefully to your critic's reply. It constitutes potentially valuable feedback, and it may alert you to possible obstacles that you (and we) have not yet considered thoroughly; so take your time and gather as much information as you can.

This objection generally gives voice to the belief that "human nature" will prevent the plan's success. Critics holding this belief are telling you that humans, including themselves possibly, are too aggressive, too greedy, too dishonest, too suspicious, too fearful, too belligerent, too short-sighted, and in general too self-serving to participate whole-heartedly in the adoption and implementation of your (and our) plan.

This is another serious criticism and as such it deserves your serious consideration. It is one with which we have wrestled for many years. For those critics seeking an excuse not to commit to our plan, it is as good as any. To them we say, "OK! Use this one. Let others test the plan." To those still open-minded we say, "Read on!"

We wish to point out that "human nature" is not a thing. You cannot put it in a wheelbarrow. It is, instead, an abstract description of human behavior. Human behavior stems from just two basic causes: genetic predisposition (instinct) and human culture (experience), both of which evolve with time.

Genetically predisposed behavior, also known as "instinct", evolves very slowly. Millions of years of evolution underlie today's human instincts. In all of recorded and archeologically derived human history there has been very little, if any, change in instinctive human behavior. And yet people take actions every day that are contradictory to human instinct.

And what is more, as seen macroscopically, human behavior has changed dramatically in just the last ten thousand years. The invention of agriculture, the invention of cities, the invention of government, the invention of printing, the inventions of science, industry, and medicine, the invention of radio communication, the invention of computers, and the invention of the Internet all have made enormous changes in day-to-day human behavior.

While the process of genetic evolution by natural selection (or otherwise) appears to be slowing down, the evolution of human behavior is clearly accelerating. How is this possible?

The answer lies in the cultural causes of human behavior. Culture, which may be thought of as humanity's collective cumulative experience, is capable of evolving very quickly, in some instances *suddenly*, as when a particularly fruitful invention becomes available. It is precisely this cultural evolution, or extragenetic evolution, that our plan seeks to maximize. It is for this reason that we refer to our ethical principles as the "Evolutionary Ethic".

To explain our undaunted optimism in the face of the "human nature" criticism, we need to develop a somewhat deeper perspective concerning this cultural evolution. For a much more detailed, yet still very readable, explanation of evolution we refer the reader to John David Garcia's book, *Creative Transformation.*

Very briefly stated, current scientific theory strongly suggests that inanimate matter evolved into life through a process, now well understood, called chemical evolution. Awareness was derived as part of this process. As life forms evolved, their level of awareness increased to the point where suddenly (among a few species) true consciousness appeared, which is to say awareness of awareness. This awareness of awareness, which we seem to share with the great apes, the cetaceans (whales, porpoises, and dolphins), and probably elephants, is what properly defines personhood. It is a necessary (though not sufficient) condition for the development of ethics, morality, and conscience.

The invention of printing made the transmission of information between past and future generations vastly easier and more effective; so the accumulated experience (culture) is now preserved and passed on much more quickly and readily. The inventions of computer and Internet vastly expand that human capability.

Just before evolution gave us awareness of awareness, and with it personhood, pre-hominid life was at a cusp in its development. The advent of consciousness was a really big deal; it made person-life into something qualitatively different from animal-life. We are at a similar cusp today, for the simple reason that we know about our own consciousness and can choose to affect the direction in which it evolves.

In a sense, we became conscious humans when we became aware of our awareness. Today we are becoming something still more wonderful, because we are becoming conscious of our consciousness. This will ultimately make it possible for us to "steer" the evolution of our evolution, both culturally and genetically. To fully realize this potential requires us to align our intentions with the evolutionary process itself. This book explains one way of doing this; there may be many others, but we have yet to discover them.

So, to the extent that our cultural evolution can now be chosen consciously, rather than imposed upon us by the slow genetic process of natural selection, human nature can now become whatever we choose it to be. This gives us hope.

There is another good reason to hope that should be mentioned when faced with a critic of the "human nature" persuasion. It is implicit in the previously mentioned success of Japanese industry. This success was achieved by applying the management principles of Dr. William E. Deming, starting in 1950.

By 1965 the Japanese had proven the validity of Dr. Deming's methodology. Not only did they transform their third-rate industry into the most successful industry on the planet, but also, they transformed the Japanese industrial workplace into an environment where the Japanese worker feels valued and appreciated. This brought excitement, loyalty, and enthusiasm to the workplace community.

Even though industrial companies in Japan continue to be organized hierarchically, they are no longer very bureaucratic. This was an enormously significant achievement.

Although the Japanese government facilitated the application of the Deming model to Japanese industry, it failed to apply the Deming model to itself (i.e. to Japanese government) and to other Japanese institutions. Their government continues, instead, to operate largely on the Samurai model, which is highly competitive, but which is much less creative than the Deming model.

This failure, or oversight, of the Japanese is hardly surprising, since the Deming model was designed for use by industries, and its proper application in other settings is not obvious. As we have proven, the Deming management model is a logical subset of the somewhat broader, and therefore more widely applicable, set of principles that we set forth in the ***Bill of Ethics***.

While the success of the Japanese experiment with the Deming model is not a definitive proof that other (than industrial) institutions will have similar success using our model, still it provides a very strong argument for the credibility of our model and for the value of experimentally applying our model to non-industrial institutions. In this way the validity of our model can be tested, its shortcomings can be discerned, and the model itself can be improved until it succeeds.

CHAPTER 16

Fleshing Out the Dream

Having a dream isn't the same thing as having a plan. So let's briefly consider some specific steps that will need to be included as we develop a full-fledged game plan. Below are just two of many available examples.

- **Start-Up:** Based on past experience, we recommend creating a HoloMat of nine Octologues to spearhead the implementation of the Titania Project. As of this writing (July 2013), the first training seminar for this step is already being planned and scheduled. The second and third seminars in the series can follow in short order. With adequate promotion, this start-up phase could be completed within a year – so this looks like our first milestone.

- **The Titanian Legal System:**
  When government by law was first invented, eight thousand years ago in Sumer, the basis of law (and hence government itself) was "might makes right". The kings and tribal chieftains who could afford to field armies saw it was to their advantage to form a ***power-brokerage cartel*** to manage their ***shared monopoly*** of power over their neighbors. The mechanism that they invented to accomplish this feat, we know today as ***hierarchy***. It is the central feature of almost all our institutions today, including those of **B**usiness, **O**rganized **R**eligion, and **G**overnment (BORG).

  Today it is generally understood, at least in the developed western world, that the "might" of military and police forces does not, in fact, confer the "right", upon those who wield such coercive power, to command the lives of those who lack these powers. Accordingly, most of the world's governments give lip-service to the notion that they exist to serve the interests of those whom they govern. And indeed, in an ethical human society, this concept would represent reality.

Unfortunately, for most of the people of the world, government that serves the interests of the public is just a myth, perpetuated by those who use the lie to facilitate their manipulation of those less resourceful than themselves. By believing the lie we permit our own enslavement.

In reality the nature of government has not changed since the days of Sumer. It remains a power-brokerage cartel that truly serves only its own interests:

o Maximization of its members' profits,

o Maximization of its powers of coercion, and

o Stabilization of its monopoly role in the power-brokerage marketplace.

The rest of society, with few and insignificant exceptions, complies with the demands of government, even to the extent of mirroring one of its worst features, the use of hierarchy as a mechanism for power-brokerage, within the structures of virtually all our institutions, both public and private.

Thus it is that humanity today labors under the burden of a vast parasite, which, left unchecked, will do what all parasites do: it will destroy its host, even though its own survival depends upon the health of its host. Today the parasite of government has the power to turn our entire planet into a radioactive cinder, unfit to sustain any kind of life as we know it. As things stand now, it is likely to do this.

But maybe it's not too late. Maybe, by using HoloMatic institutions comprised of ethical Octologues, we can pull ourselves back from the brink of disaster and transform human society into a sustainable thriving whole.

Whether you are a legislator, a judge (active or retired), an attorney (practicing or not), a paralegal, or merely a justice-minded law student, your participation in the development of Titania, your personal effort, your creativity could be crucial to the future of humanity itself.

To understand what is needed, let's take a quick look at what is wrong with our current legal systems. Such systems today, the world over, are prone to the following obvious flaws, foibles, or weaknesses:

1. Many laws forbid ethical acts.

2. Many laws require unethical acts.

3. Many laws take money, property, financial opportunity, privacy, or freedom away from those to whom it belongs and bestow it upon those to whom it does not belong.

4. Many laws, regardless of their merit, are passed by legislators to curry favor with voters or with the lobbyists who pay for their election campaigns.

5. Many laws continue to be enforced long after it is obvious that they do not produce the behavioral results that they were intended to produce – or even when they produce the *opposite* effects.

6. Many laws are passed and enforced in the name of "protecting the public" when, in fact, they primarily serve to give a group of influential people protection against the market encroachment of another, less influential, group of people. In this the public is the loser.

7. Many judges openly forbid jurors from considering the merits or legitimacy of the laws being enforced in their courtrooms. This serves to bureaucratize the legal system by immunizing it against corrective feedback. In this case everyone is the loser.

8. To be legitimate, by modern standards, a law must serve the best interests of the people – all the people – who are supposedly being protected by the law. When this principle is violated, the resulting law is not legitimate and cannot be ethically enforced.

9. Enactment of a law is, by its nature, a delegation of authority from the legislators enacting the law to the legislative body that those individual legislators comprise. When a group of legislators enact a law that delegates authority that those legislators do not possess **as individuals**, the resulting law is not legitimate and cannot be ethically enforced.

10. Mindful of the fact that governments are power-brokerage cartels whose true purposes are purely self-serving, it is clear that laws that support and/or enforce the true purposes of government are never ethical. The vast majority of laws in the world today fall into this category.

From the foregoing description of the "Foibles" of government-enacted law, and from what we have shown elsewhere concerning the Evolutionary Ethic and the "Comforting Lies", we can draw the following logical conclusions, which comprise some of the principles of just law:

1. Government, as we know it, is incapable of enacting and/or enforcing just (ethical) laws.

2. Political systems, at best, determine who gets to participate in the power-brokerage cartels that we call "governments"; but nothing in any political process enables the people governed to alter the unethical nature of government. Majority Rule contributes to this fact.

3. For a society to thrive it must have a legal system that is entirely independent of government.

4. Such a legal system must be privately funded and privately operated by a group of people committed to the principles of just (ethical) law.

5. Just laws must be enacted solely to serve the ends defined by the **Evolutionary Ethic** or an alternative ethic that is the logical equivalent of the **Evolutionary Ethic**, and must be further constrained to embody the principle that ethical ends can only be achieved by means that are ethical ends in themselves.

6. Any law, rule, regulation, or procedure sanctioned by the *Bill of Ethics* qualifies as an artifact or embodiment of just law.

7. Any law, rule, regulation, or procedure not sanctioned by the *Bill of Ethics* is not an artifact or embodiment of just

law.

8. For a society to thrive, its unjust laws and the rules, regulations, and procedures that support and enforce them must be repealed.

9. The exercise of (coercive) power over others is never ethical except in the case of the defense of self or others against unethical acts – and then only when all available non-coercive means have failed – and even then limited to the application of the minimum amount of coercive force required to prevent further occurrence of the unethical act or to provide redress of the harm done by the unethical act or acts already perpetrated.

It is the intention of the **Titania Project** to create and operate an alternative legal system to which the public can turn for the arbitration of conflicts, the redress of grievances, and the establishment and enforcement of just laws. To that end:

1. The Titanian Legal System (TLS) will be built upon the definitions and principles provided by the ***Bill of Ethics.***

2. The TLS will be privately owned and operated, entirely independent of government, and will be funded entirely by voluntary payment of service fees and subscriptions by persons wishing to avail themselves of the services afforded by the TLS.

3. Organizational elements of the TLS will be structured as HoloMats of Octologues according to the definitions provided by the Constitution of **Titania**.

4. Over time, and as its means permit, the TLS will define and codify just law in the fields of contracts, business, torts, the environment, and criminal law.

5. On the same basis, the TLS will offer services that may include, but not be limited to the following:

a. Mediation,
b. Arbitration,
c. Education,
d. Consultation,
e. Expert testimony,
f. Judicial services, such as:

    1) Defense of persons unjustly accused of criminal charges under government-enacted laws in government courts.

    2) The writing of legal briefs arguing for the repeal of unjust laws and the redress of grievances for persons against whom unjust laws have been enforced.

    3) Development of a system of legal defenses against the enforcement of any and all laws providing for the practice of taxation by government at all levels, and against all laws forbidding *mala prohibita*.

    4) Development of a system whereby an ethical public can delegate its self-defense rights to an ethically constituted enforcement HoloMat.

    5) Development of a set of truly ethical standards for dealing with cases of *mala in se*, together with guidelines for actions by police, courts, and "correc-

tions" systems endeavoring to protect the public from society's predators and parasites, including those in government.

Development of the TLS can begin within six months of startup and continue as an ongoing Titanian project.

~~~|~~~

The Titanian Education System

Today's educational system exists for just two purposes:

1. To force job applicants to pay the expenses involved in demonstrating their competence to prospective employers – even though the employers will be the ones to profit from the employee's work, and

2. To train the public from an early age to accept as truth the Comforting Lies that support the *status quo* – thereby ensuring our compliance with unjust edicts that masquerade as laws in our society.

These are clearly not ethical purposes, as they further the exploitation of employees and the control of the public at large. An ethical educational system, by contrast, must exist to enhance the creativity of the students by stimulating their curiosity and providing for the satisfaction of that curiosity.

Since rewards and punishments hinder creativity and limit curiosity, testing, ranking, and grading of students' performance should only occur on a voluntary basis, allowing students feedback on their level of competence in any subject. The results of such diagnostics should only be available to the students, their parents (if they are minors), and those individuals with whom the individual students wish to share such information. Testing will, under no circumstances, be mandatory.

A HoloMatically organized education system can provide for an endless range of experimental programs, innovative approaches, and geographically local variations that will allow for the system to be continuously improved.

Since getting a job on graduation will no longer be an objective of education, graduation will no longer be a needed feature of the system. Instead, the system can provide an extremely broad lifelong learning curriculum that continuously enhances the student's creativity while fostering a committed respect for the Evolutionary Ethic and its resulting principles.

The general adoption of the Titanian Education Model could catalyze a whole new Human Renaissance, with advantages and opportunities for all that are barely imaginable today. Time Frame: Six months to get started / Five years to be humanity's dominant educational modality.

PART 4

Stories for Your Right Brain

CHAPTER 17

The Legend of Odoka, The Castle Builder

Once upon a time, long ago - or maybe not so long ago, in a land far away - or maybe not so far away, there lived a brave and ambitious little boy named Odoka. Two things were very unusual about Odoka. First, he knew as soon as he could walk that he would one day accomplish great things in his life; that he would one day be admired and respected by others. And second, and this is the really unusual part, he expected too that he would one day have enemies... and that these enemies would someday attack him. So he resolved early in his life to build himself a fortified castle.

Odoka was still just a child when he first built a castle. He built it on a beach near his home; and since it was free and plentiful he built it of sand. Unlike other children his age he understood that only wet sand has any strength, so he went to great lengths to see to it that his walls and towers and turrets were always moist and firm. He also understood that the sea could wash away his castle; so he built it well above the highest level that the tide could reach. He arranged for his moat to be filled and his castle to be moistened by a small stream that he diverted for these purposes. It was a beautiful castle.

One day when he was almost finished building his castle a young man, about his father's age, happened by and watched him for a while as he was adding crenellations to the tops of his battlements.

"A good day to you young master!" said the man. "That's a fine castle you're building there; and very innovative too."

"Thank you sir." said Odoka, for he had been taught to be a polite and respectful child.

"Do you think", said the man, "that you could use some help with it?"

"Oh, no sir. Though I thank you kindly", said Odoka. I know just what I'm doing and I have the project quite in hand, if you know what I mean."

"That's great!" said the man with a smile. "I wish you the best of luck with it." And with that he turned and went on his way.

Well, it was just that night that the weather turned stormy and the wind blew hard out of the west as if it wanted to knock the trees down - in fact it did knock a few down. And it rained so hard the streams rose and flooded some of the low-lying areas. And in the morning when Odoka went to see how his castle had fared he could barely recognize the spot where it had been. What hadn't blown away on the wind had been washed bare by the flooded stream. He sat down, discouraged - though by no means defeated.

The next time Odoka built a castle he was already a grown man. In fact he had already had some notable accomplishments; had a reputation for helping people; and in doing so had made some enemies.

On this occasion he decided to build his castle of tree trunks. We might relate to it as a western style stockade. Finding a suitable site well supplied with trees he applied himself in his usual energetic manner; soon erecting a sturdy structure of notched and interlocking timbers designed to stand firmly against all foreseeable challenges. The walls of this castle fairly bristled with sharpened wooden shafts to discourage climbers and secure battle stations studded the periphery of the walls at regular intervals. It was an impressive sight by any estimate.

One day, as Odoka was putting the finishing touches on his defense system an older man came by and admired his handiwork. "This is a great looking castle!" said the man. "But what do you plan to do if your attackers set it on fire?"

Thanks," said Odoka, "I've got it all planned out. I've diverted a stream and installed a sprinkler system so that I can put out a fire on any section of the castle by just turning a valve. I expect it to work quite handily."

You sure have a great imagination", said the older man. "Could you use some help with the final plans for this wonderful creation of yours?"

I really appreciate your offer", said Odoka, "but I know what I'm doing and really think I have the project well in hand."

Well, I sure wish you luck with it", said the smiling visitor. "I suspect you might need it." And without a further word of explanation he turned on his heel and left the way he had come.

As fate would have it, it was only the day after the completion of Odoka's castle when his enemies did, in fact, attack him in his fortress. And perhaps it was no great surprise when they shot burning arrows at the stockade and set it on fire at numerous locations along its circumference.

Certainly the attackers were surprised when Odoka, smiling grimly, turned on his sprinkler system and began putting out the fires, first along one section of the wall, and then another. In the end it was Odoka who was most surprised when his attackers found and rediverted the stream that supplied his water; so his sprinkler system suddenly ran dry. Later that day his enemies succeeded in burning the fortress to the ground.

Fortunately, Odoka managed to escape with his life. And a few days later he could be seen sitting amid the ashes of his castle, very discouraged - though by no means defeated. His loss certainly set him to thinking.

The third castle that Odoka built was made of bricks. He had found a building site near a plentiful supply of clay and had devised a brick-making machine that allowed him to turn out bricks at a prodigious rate. A vigorous and mature man by now, Odoka was determined not to be blown out, flooded out, or burned out of his castle again. Bricks, he had learned, were the hardest and most durable building material known to man, just as they are today. So, brick was the substance of choice for this important project.

Well, it didn't take too long before the castle began to take shape. It was gorgeous. Taking full advantage of the flexibility afforded by the medium of brick, Odoka was able to build a structure that was both strong and attractive; almost intricate. Besides crenellations, his fortress walls were emblazoned with archery slots, hot oil sluices, deadfalls, inverted stairs, and a panoply of traps and pitfalls to distract the unwary attacker. It was by far his best architectural creation to date.

This time Odoka was *not* visited by an older man on the eve of his enemies' attack. So the attack came as more of a surprise than it might otherwise have been. As his foes attempted to overcome his defenses Odoka proved himself many times over to be a valiant man of action. He shot arrows from his archery slots, poured hot oil from his oil sluices, and activated all the snares, traps, pits, and deadfalls that he had designed so laboriously. So effective was he that he almost won.

But in the end he was unable to combat his enemies' catapults and battering machines. There were just too many of them. And the brick walls were susceptible. They crumbled and fell first at one spot, then, as he bravely defended that spot, at others. Finally he managed to escape with his life, but not with his proud arrogance; for that day it died.

A few days later Odoka was sitting on a siege engine abandoned by his enemies amid the ruins of his castle and was in deep despair. For the first time in his life he wondered if perhaps he *had* been defeated. And at this most vulnerable moment a somewhat elderly, though still vigorous, man appeared on horseback before him.

Dismounting, the visitor greeted Odoka courteously saying, "Greetings, Young Sir! I am truly sorry to find you so troubled this day. I came by last week and admired your beautiful castle immensely. In fact, I had thought to have a chat with you about the relationship between brick walls and siege engines, but you were too busy to take any notice of me so I rode on by. What a pity!"

To these words Odoka did not reply. He just looked at the older man and bit his lip as tears welled up in his eyes.

"Tell me", said the older man. "Would it mangle your pride too much to let an older fellow teach you the right way to go about this business?"

Sir", replied Odoka, "my pride has stood in my way for far too long. Since I have only this moment decided that I am not yet defeated I would be grateful for any instruction you could give me that would enable me to succeed at this outcome of mine. What is more, I will pay you any price you require that is within my power to pay, if only my success will be assured."

That's quite a commitment", said the older gentleman; "and I'll take you up on it for sure, though the price may be higher than you imagine. My name is Oyanitu, but most folks call me, 'Doc'; so you may also. Let's get started."

So began a long and dangerous journey by the two men; but, except for the bond that formed between them and the mentorship that began in this setting, the adventures of that journey are the fabric of another story altogether.

One day, though, late in the afternoon the two men rode over the crest of a mountain ridge and facing the east they beheld an amazing sight on the next mountain across the valley from them. There, glowing in the sunlight that streamed over their shoulders was the most magnificent castle Odoka had ever conceived. In fact it was beyond anything he could have imagined.

The mountain facing them was essentially a flat-topped escarpment with a sheer face dropping a thousand feet or more into a deep river flowing swiftly along the foot of the cliff. The whole visible face of this cliff had been carved into a fortified wall and polished like a gemstone. It abounded with an amazing variety of windows and terraces each overhanging the sheer drop below. As they drew nearer Odoka could see that if approached by boat the cliff face was too smooth for any purchase or handhold to grasp.

The only real entry passage was led into the face of the wall by a bridge of solid stone blocks cut perfectly smooth and joined almost seamlessly into one flawless structure. Straddling the bridge was a five hundred foot tall guard tower that looked as if it had literally grown out of the face of the cliff. It too had surfaces of polished granite as smooth as a mirror. And beneath its menacing bulk Odoka could see huge metallic gates that were several feet thick and designed to lock together so perfectly as to show no seam when closed. They stood open now as the two men approached.

What is this place, Doc?" asked Odoka in a tone that revealed the depth to which he felt overwhelmed by the impression the fortress made on him. "And to whom does it belong?"

"It is my home", grinned Oyanitu.. "It's mine, you might say. It's called, 'Syzygy'. Let me show you around."

Several hours later as the two men rested and ate in the older man's private quarters, Odoka was more stunned than ever. The castle had proven to be a veritable city delved into the native rock of the mesa. Seemingly immune to attack by ground forces the castle "roof", the top of the mesa, was a fortified farmland unapproachable except through the great halls of Syzygy because of the steep cliffs rising from the mesa's eastern boundary into the rugged mountains beyond. So few were the possible descent routes out of the mountains and onto the mesa, that it would be a simple matter for an armed force to make them impassable.

What is more, Odoka had found the interior of Syzygy to be even more beautiful than the outer view of it. Great hallways, shops, eating places, meeting rooms and entertainment centers were all thoughtfully decorated and lavishly equipped. And the building was teeming with people. They were attractive, healthy, happy seeming people.

"Do you really think, Doc, that I could someday have a castle as grand as this?" asked Odoka.

"I don't doubt it for a minute", said Oyanitu.

"What do I have to do to get started?" queried the younger man.

"Well", said Oyanitu, "you have to learn the technologies of heat and light, metal and stone. I think I'd start with cutting stone."

"All right!" said Odoka jumping up from the comfort of the couch he had been resting on. "I'm ready!"

So, for some weeks thereafter, or maybe they were months, the two men labored together in the work areas of Syzygy. Quarrying stone, smelting steel, fabricating energy sources, and generally teaching Odoka the basics of appropriately scaled architectural engineering.

Finally one day the younger man's impatience overcame his dedication. He had to go out and get started on his own castle. But before leaving he arranged to have a final briefing with his mentor.

"Odoka, have you decided just how big a castle you plan to build?"

"Yes I have", said the student. "Now that I understand the technology I'm determined to build one even bigger and better than this one".

"Have you figured out how long it will take you to build?"

"No, not yet."

"Why don't you take a few minutes to just calculate the volume of stone you will have to excavate and the time it will take you to cut that stone. Use the time figures you generated in our last stone-working session as a basis."

"All right", said Odoka and began scribbling numbers furiously on a pad of paper. "This can't be right", he groaned a few minutes later. "My calculations say it will take me five hundred years just to do the general excavation, without any time allowed for smoothing and polishing."

"That sounds about right", said Oyanitu.

"But I'll never finish", said Odoka sitting down heavily in discouragement.

"Well of course", said the elder, "there's a trick to it."

"What's that", sighed Odoka visibly relieved.

"You don't do it alone."

"Well of course! I knew that. It will only take me a few minutes to figure out how many people I need to find who want to help me build my castle. No big deal"

"Are you ready then?", asked Oyanitu.

"You bet!" said Odoka and began preparing somewhat reluctantly to depart.

A year later Odoka returned to Syzygy more discouraged than ever. Oyanitu had never seen him look so dejected.

"Odoka, my young friend what is wrong? You left here so confidently it grieves me to see you so down at the mouth."

"There's another 'trick' you forgot to tell me, Doc." said the younger man, who by now had a trace of gray in his dark hair. "How do you get people to volunteer for a project like mine? I haven't found a single person who wants to help me build my castle. I know you know the answer because you have the castle to prove it."

"I'd have told you", of course, said Oyanitu with a quiet smile. "But the last time I saw you, you didn't seem to want any more input from me. Naturally I respect you enough not to try to teach you what you don't want to learn."

"Well, I'm asking", said Odoka with some embarrassment. "How do you do it?"

"I'm going to tell you", said Oyanitu. "But since this is the last crucial piece of information that you need it is time for me now to claim the price of my help. You remember the bargain we made; the steep price I said I would exact from you for my help?"

"I haven't forgotten. What is your price?"

"I'll get to that – but first your information. The trick is that you do not ask people to help build your castle."

"I don't?" said Odoka in confusion. "But I thought you said..."

"I said you don't build alone. The trick is you ask people to help you build *their* castle."

"Th-their castle?" stammered Odoka.

"Yes, of course! Haven't you noticed all the other people who live here with me in Syzygy? Those are the people who helped me build *my* castle. It's just as much theirs as mine. I just organized the effort by finding people who want to live in a castle enough to actually *work* at it - rather than just *talk* about it."

Shame-faced for not having caught on sooner Odoka took a deep breath and asked, "So what do I owe you for all this much-needed help. No price is too much. I meant that!"

The next morning Odoka bid his old friend farewell after spending half the night learning of the price he was to pay for the old man's help. There was no question that the task was difficult beyond belief. But he had made a commitment and you know how tenaciously he went about things.

So now he began a solo journey of some weeks, or maybe years, and eventually found a suitable site for his own castle. And by now he had met quite a number of people who seriously wanted to live in a castle; and they joined him on the work site.

Slow at first, the work on the great castle went faster and faster as he and his partners gained greater skill and attracted still more participants. And eventually the work was done. It was utterly magnificent! Even the fortress, Syzygy, was not a match for Odoka's creation. He and all his partners held a great housewarming party and even Oyanitu and a few of his household journeyed there to take part in it.

Not long after, on a warm summer day Odoka set out to begin paying his debt to his old friend. With a light pack on his horse's rump he set off down the lane in the woodlands that abutted his group's property. The sun was shining on the trees about him and the world seemed to have a moist green smell, as if the land itself was approving what he was about to do.

In the distance, drawing gradually nearer, he could hear the distinctive sound of an axe biting into the wood of a tall tree. He urged his horse eagerly into a trot. In what seemed moments he caught sight of what he was looking for. His informants had apparently given him accurate information.

In a clearing before him, just off the lane, a young man labored with his shirt off in the warm sun. His skin was deeply tanned from spending long days at such efforts. About him were piled stacks of logs some notched together into regular shapes, others sharpened at one end or both. A pattern of stakes in the ground marked out where construction was about to occur.

"Hi there, Young Fellow", called Odoka, smiling as he rode into the clearing and reined in his horse. "If I'm not mistaken you're starting to build yourself a right handsome castle out of all these logs. Is that right?"

"Sure is!" said the young man. "And it's coming along just according to plan", said the youth obviously pleased with himself.

"Well now", said Odoka stepping down from his saddle, "Do you think you could use some help with this project of yours?"

CHAPTER 18

THE REAL STORY OF MOSES AND THE TEN SUGGESTIONS

As Recorded by Adam Kadmon

in the

Salton Sea Scroll

Edited by Robert E. Podolsky

The Real Story of Moses and the Ten Suggestions As Related by Adam Kadmon

As I record these words our leader, Moses, just returned from the Mountain of Wonder, is telling our people the story of his sojourn with God during which Moses was given the stone tablets which reveal God's will concerning his people. For three days and nights I have sat with him in his tent with the flaps closed while the people awaited the news of his journey. To me he said, "Adam Kadmon, it is to you that I will tell my story first; for I know you and trust you to report it accurately. In the years to come many will tell it the way they wish I had said it, rather than as it really was. So heed my words and record them truly."

Thus it is to me that the great honor has befallen of recording truly for all future generations the tale of Moses' conversation with the Great One; so here it is, in his own words even as he spoke them to me.

Long have we wandered in the wilderness hoping the Great One would lead us to a fertile and hospitable land that we could call our own. But we seem to be as far from that dream today as the day we left the kingdom of Pharaoh. So it is that I decided to climb to the heights of the nearby Mountain of Wonder, there to fast, to consider our plight, and to ask God's help in drawing this long and perilous journey to a successful conclusion.

On my trek up the mountainside I bethought myself as to the nature of our plight and came to the realization that we have thus far proven unworthy of God's more generous blessings. We despoil the land through which we travel. We treat one another harshly and with indifference to the caring that we seemed to share while we were in bondage. Sometimes violence breaks out amidst our disputes, which seem to be more common than in years past. Many of us seem inclined to return to a more primitive faith; in our minds populating the world with all manner of gods and demons and making sacrifice to images and statues in hopes of placating the wrath of unknown spirits. Our husbandry of our meager resources fails to improve and our arts and our crafts languish. Little wonder God is not pleased with us! My path lies plain before me. I must ask God how we can change to become more worthy in his eyes.

I was still thinking along these lines when I arrived at the upland plateau that lies just below the peak of the great mountain. There, looking out over the land below, I noted the sun was almost setting; yet there seemed no reason to delay. So I knelt beneath the sky and lifted my voice to the heavens.

"Oh, Great God of heaven and earth," I cried, "I would speak with you concerning the fate of my people, your children suffering the exile of the desert. Will you hear my plea?" Then the sky shook and the ground trembled and a great stern voice spoke to me.

"Moses, my young friend, how good it is to see you again! Do you suppose you could find time to visit me more often; or would that be asking too much?"

Stunned by the implied rebuke I cried, "Dear God, how is it that your words sound so much like the greetings I so often received from my mother?"

Softening somewhat the voice responded, *"I thought a familiar greeting might set you at ease somewhat under these rather daunting circumstances. I see I was mistaken. Forgive me."*

"Of course, Great One. If you truly want to ease my anxiety it would help if I could see you; as I am unaccustomed to holding conversations with a disembodied voice."

"Well," God answered, *"I might be able to help you out. How would you wish me to appear? I have some flexibility in this matter."*

"Any image will do," I said, "to focus my attention; though perhaps it would be best if it were one that combined something ordinary with something unmistakably out of the ordinary." As I said this I was thinking that it could be risky if God appeared too ordinary. I might behave too familiarly toward him and offend him in some unforeseen way.

"Okay," said God, *"I'll speak to you as a burning bush as I did at our last meeting. Will that suit you?"*

"Yes, of course," I said. And as I did the bush a few feet to my left appeared to burst into flame; strange purple flame with a pale blue shimmer in the air surrounding it. And rather than being consumed by the flame I noticed the bush seemed to enjoy the presence of the flame. Still more unusual was the fact that I could sense the obvious pleasure the bush was experiencing.

"Will this do?," asked the bush in God's voice.

"Perfectly!" I replied. "Uh...uh...hmmm. God, would it be all right with you if before we get to the serious discussion that brought me here, could I ask you a few lesser questions that have been on my mind for some time?"

"Not at all, Moses. Take your time. In fact, if it's all right with you I'll just shift us outside of time while we have our chat, so we can take as long as you like and it won't be deducted from your time in life."

"Great," I said; though I didn't really understand the offer. But I'm not one to turn down a possible benefit deriving from God, himself. "My first question is, 'Are you really male or female?'"

Now the voice seemed to smile. ***"Neither. I'm too big to be either one alone. And I reproduce asexually."*** As I was deciding whether or not to inquire further concerning his reproductive modality he offered, ***"In case you were wondering, I reproduce by selecting hospitable planets, like yours, here and there in the Universe and by creating people-species like you who have the potential to transform themselves into beings like me."***

Feeling a little overwhelmed by what I took to be some of the possible implications of what I had just heard, I ventured to ask, "Wait a minute now. What exactly do you mean when you use the word, 'Universe'?"

"Well", he said, "the Universe is everything that exists within the reach of the light from your oil lamp. It includes everything living or inanimate on your world, everything you can see in the heavens including the sun, the moon, the stars, and the planets; and it includes a vast region encompassing numbers of additional suns, moons, and planets so great that the human mind cannot conceive them."

"All right; I can understand that," I said. "So, what do you mean by 'people-species'?"

"'People or persons,' as I use the term, are members of a very special kind of species; one that has awareness of its own awareness. As a person you know that you are separate from your surroundings. There is 'you' and there is 'not-you'. As you interact with your environment you know that you are having feelings, thoughts and perceptions in response to the not-you that is around you. Is that clear?"

"Very," I replied. "So are you saying that you reproduce by scattering person-hood around the Universe and that each person can somehow become a god like You?"

"Not exactly," he responded. *"Human beings are currently too short-lived for such a personal achievement. But I have in fact endowed you with the ability to aspire to such growth. And if*

enough of you entertain such aspirations, eventually your species could transform itself into a being like me. Thus will I be reproduced, if my creation of you was good and if you choose to continue your evolution."

"I notice that you use the words, 'creation' and 'evolution' in the same breath. Which is it? Are humans created or evolved? Some of my people get into violent disputes about this; so I really need to know."

"Well," said God, *"have you ever seen a beautiful leather saddle; one with elaborate patterns and designs carved or tooled into the leather?"*

"Surely," said I.

"Would you say that saddle was 'created' by the saddle-maker, or was it 'tooled'?"

"Well, both of course."

"And do you think less of the saddle-maker because he uses tools?"

"Of course not!"

"Exactly," said God. *"And so it is with my creation of the Universe, including humanity. I used evolution as the primary tool to accomplish the task."*

I thought about this information for several minutes and realized that some among my people might ask me the question that was forming in my mind; so it seemed important to ask it. "So what exactly *is* 'evolution' anyway."

"To answer that question let's start with the notion of the polarity between order and chaos. Take the structure of wood, for example. If you look at it closely enough you see it has a very organized internal structure. You might say it's very orderly. But when you burn it you destroy most of that orderliness and replace it with smoke and ash which are much less orderly; much more chaotic. Is that making sense to you?"

"I guess so; but I'm not sure what you are getting at."

"That's all right. Bear with me a little longer and it should all come clear. I built the Universe in such a way that if one isolates a region of space that contains matter the orderliness of that matter can only diminish; and the chaos of it can only increase. Someday humankind will likely discover that because of this it is possible for them to make wonderful machines. They will probably call this fact the 'second law of thermodynamics'."

"Amazing," I said, "will I live to see the day?"

"I doubt it," said God, *"but it is good that you know about it anyway. Now we come finally to the answer to your question about evolution. The most amazing thing about the Universe is the fact that there are sizable areas where almost nothing is isolated. For instance, here on your world almost everything gets bathed in sunlight every day.*

So the sea and the atmosphere are not constrained to always become more chaotic and less orderly. Under these conditions there are areas where chaos diminishes and order increases. And that is the fundamental nature of evolution."

"Is that it," I asked – "The whole 'magilla'?[6] Why would anyone be upset or argue about that?"

"That simple fact has consequences," he said lowering his voice to an almost conspiratorial tone. *"To create life I just created energy and matter and gave them the necessary properties; and let them go. Those properties were the 'commands' that made everything else in the Universe unfold like a flower. First the things you see in the sky evolved from the raw materials that I provided. Then matter evolved into what we call 'life'. It was characterized mainly by a much higher level of awareness than was exhibited by all the preceding forms of energy and matter. And of course it was much more highly organized and ordered and much less chaotic.*

The next stage of evolution was the appearance of consciousness. Consciousness, which we sometimes call 'sentience', is nothing but awareness of one's own awareness. We mentioned that before when we talked about what makes people differ-

---

[6] " Magilla, or more properly megillah, comes from the Hebrew word 'megillah' which refers specifically to the book of Esther (traditionally read in the synagogue during the festival of Purim) or to that of Ruth. From there is has been generalised to mean anything long and detailed (and ultimately boring) - Esther is filled with tiny details, recounted one on top of the other. The 'whole megilleh' thus means the whole boring rigmarole." – From wordwizard.com

ent from other life-forms. Very soon now, in just five thousand years or so, humankind will probably be ready for the next stage of evolution, in which awareness becomes so great that it becomes possible for humans to take charge of their own evolution; to steer it so to speak. In a sense it will be the beginning of the evolution of evolution. When that happens, many wonderful and terrible possibilities will become available to your species. Becoming like me is one of them."

"How woooonderful!" I practically sang. "What a grand future to work toward!" I opined, practically jumping up and down. "Can anyone really object to such a blessed world-view?"

"Moses," said God, *"haven't you noticed that there are many people who take pleasure in asserting their dominance over others?"*

"Egypt's Pharaoh is a pretty good example."

"Some people like to believe that I 'micro-manage' their lives twenty-four hours a day; and the reality is that I don't; that I wouldn't want to under any circumstances. The way I created the Universe is a good example of how I operate. I just put all the ingredients in place, commanded the laws that govern it all, and went away and let life happen."

"That seems to be turning out to have been a viable plan," I ventured.

"Viable, indeed!" **said God.** *"The fact is you don't need me to be looking over your shoulder all the time. Nor do you need the service of priests to intercede for you with me; you can address me directly by seeking answers from within yourselves and within my works."*

"In years to come there will be many people who, like Pharaoh, will persuade the masses about them that they are somehow closer to me than those multitudes are; that to live well it is necessary to receive the approval of this priesthood. The falsehood of these lies is apparent if one understands that I let evolution take its course and don't interfere in the details of people's lives. If people knew how indifferent I am to them individually they would accord no special respect to the self-designated priesthood; and the priesthood would have no power. The disputes about creation and evolution that you have observed among your followers is the beginning of this phenomenon. It is simply a power struggle for control of people's minds, hearts, and resources. As long as this power struggle continues there will always be some kind of priesthood to claim a special share of the products of others' creativity."

"Well," I said, "This seems to bring me to my underlying concern, the main question to which I need an answer. My people have wandered in the desert with me for a long time. I thought by now we would have found our ancient homeland and begun enjoying a more settled life. Yet still we wander aimlessly. It seems to me that we are being punished for being unworthy of your blessings. So, God, what must we do to be worthy of you?"

"Ah, Moses; if I had feelings I would be so sad hearing you ask me that! Don't you know...you already have my blessings. All humankind has my blessings; fully and without reservations. I have put in your hands everything you need to have anything you want in life and more still than you have ever dreamed."

Stunned, I dropped to the ground and pondered the Great One's words. Somehow I had gotten it all wrong. We were *not* being punished; we were blessed beyond my fondest dreams. 'If he gave us the blessings and we were still suffering', I reasoned, 'our fate must be in our own hands, not his'. This seemed consistent with what he had said previously about creating an evolving universe and then leaving it alone. To be sure I understood I asked, "God, are you saying that all we have to do to find the 'Promised Land' is to make certain choices about how we use the resources that you have already given us?"

"Almost," he answered. **"I never said you would 'find' the Promised Land. If you recall I said you would 'obtain' the Promised Land. What is more it was a mistake to think I was referring to your people's ancient homeland. You are now ready to understand that I meant you would create a new homeland through your own efforts. A far better one than your people have ever known before."**

"Our own efforts....?" I was incredulous and awe-struck at one and the same time. Then it came to me in a flash. The only new information we need is the 'how'. How could we go about creating the Promised Land - to maximize the likelihood of our success. So I asked, "Great One, are you willing to tell us how to do this wonderful feat?"

"Of course," he replied. *"Did you think I would put you through all this only to tease you? I've been waiting for you to ask the question." "Whenever you are ready, I'll tell all. I will give you a single instruction which I know you are capable of following, and if you choose to use it fully your people and your species will have everything you could dream of having."*

"Well," said I, "I'm ready now; or I will be as soon as I find a way to record your instruction. I want to take it to my people and tell them it is your commandment. Then they will really take it seriously."

"I'll record it for you; but you must understand it is not a commandment, merely a suggestion."

"But...but...," I stammered, "surely my people will take it more to heart if you command us to obey it." I hazarded.

At this the burning bush *smiled visibly* and God said, *"If I made it a commandment I would create a paradox, for you would be unable to obey it."*

"Now you have lost me," I complained. "Why, exactly, can't it be a commandment?"

"First, said God, let me show you what it is." At this the bush brightened and a beam of light shot from it upon the ground before me; and before I

could blink twice the beam of light carved a large stone tablet out of the solid rock. Incised into the upper right-hand corner of it in the language of my people were the finely engraved words,

> **"God's Number One Suggestion: To the best of your ability, be like me."**

While my eyes returned to normal I thought about the inscription. "That's wonderful, God; but what does it mean? Should we seek to be powerful and awe-inspiring? Should we try to carve stone with light? What does it mean to be 'like you'?"

"I thought you might ask that," said God, "That's why I left so much room on the tablet." Again the beam of light flashed, and when I could see again the tablet read,

> "God's Number One Suggestion: To the best of your ability be like me: love truth above all else; increase the awareness of all people; nurture creativity and personal evolution in yourself and others; and harm no one except to prevent them from harming yourself or others."

Still unsure why the words before me were not to be a commandment, I began to grapple with the seemingly simple concepts that it contained. "That part about loving truth," I said, "What truth are we talking about. Should I love Pharaoh's truth that says he is the center of everything?"

"No.," he said, *"I am referring to the only truth that really matters in the greater scheme of things. That's objective truth; truth that can be tested by more than one person. The more a truth has been tested the wiser you are to love it."*

"All right," said I, "how does one test truth?"

"To answer that question, I have to introduce you to the concept of 'intelligence'; which is the ability to predict and control events in the world about you; or, to put it another way, it is one's ability to initiate and maintain causal relationships between events that you are in a position to influence."

"Can you give me a 'for instance'?" I asked.

"Surely. Suppose you stand with a friend on a high ledge; and each of you holds a stone in your hand. The stones are of the same size and shape; but yours weighs twice as much as the one your friend holds. He is going to drop his stone off the ledge. You wish for some reason to drop your stone in such a way that it reaches the ground below at the same time as his. The two stones striking the ground at the same time is the event you want to cause by releasing your stone at the proper time. Thus a measure of your intelligence. is your ability to form the proper causal relationship between the event where you release your stone and the event where the stones hit the ground below at the same instant. Clear so far?"

"Yes," I said, picturing the falling stones in my mind.

"So what does your intuitive personal inner truth tell you that you will have to do? Will you drop your stone before your friend drops his; after he drops his; or at the same time?"

"After." said I. "Being heavier, my stone will fall faster; so I'll give his stone a head start if the two are to arrive together."

"Now for the test. You and your friend drop some stones and note the results. After a certain number of trials you conclude that all stones of the same size and shape fall at the same speed, regardless of their weight. Surprise! Objective truth is often at odds with intuitive or personal truth."

"Now we can understand the difference between objective truth and objective falsehood. When you believed you had to give the lighter stone a head start, did that belief increase or decrease your intelligence?"

"It obviously decreased it."

"And had you believed that objects that differ only in their weight would fall at the same speed, what would have been the result?"

"That would have increased my intelligence."

"So," concluded God, *"to finally answer your question: we test the objective truth of a statement by noting whether belief in the statement's truth in-*

creases or decreases our intelligence. Belief in truth increases intelligence; and belief in falsehood diminishes intelligence."

"That seems very clear and easy to grasp," I said. "I think I'm ready to get back to your 'Suggestion'. You say 'nurture creativity...' I think I know what that means intuitively; but to be on the safe side I'd like you tell me more precisely what it means."

"Very well," said God, "creativity is the act or tendency to act in ways that reveal new objective truths."

At this point I realized I was missing an important piece of the mosaic that was being shown me. So I asked abruptly, "How does art fit into the scheme of things? Its truth isn't objective. You have me worried here."

"I am glad to see you are paying attention!" said God, *"Art is good. We test new information to see if it is true. But the process by which we acquire new information is not objective. Art is the precursor of new information. It is an essential part of the creative process, and therefore very valuable."*

"All right," I said, "are you ready to tell me why your suggestion isn't a commandment and why if you made it a commandment I would be unable to obey it?"

Again the burning bush seemed to smile, and God said, *"Ready indeed. Just reason along with me here using the information I have already given you. For starters, my commands are always obeyed. Go back to the exercise of dropping rocks to see how fast they fall. You will find the rocks always fall the same way. No exceptions. Rocks don't have a choice in the matter. Would you want humans to be like the rocks...choiceless toys that dance at my will?"*

I started to reply but God went on as if he knew my answer, *"Surely I could arrange for humans to always be friendly and polite to one another; but then they wouldn't have free will; they would no longer be humans. For that matter, in order to do this and to impose my will upon you and your kind I would have to make you unaware of your awareness. This would be an evolutionary step backward. If I did such a thing it would be inconsistent with the suggestion that I gave you. If I command you to seek personal evolution I will take away the highest evolutionary achievement your species has attained. Can you see the paradox in that?"*

With more than a little regret I conceded that God was right in his understanding of the situation. As awkward as it might be for me, I was really asking God to act ungodly when I sought a command instead of a suggestion. If my people were ever to aspire to godliness we would need all the awareness we could acquire. I gave in. "You're right of course. What else could I expect of God?," I said. At this point I looked down again at the tablet and contemplated God's Suggestion.

> "God's Number One Suggestion: To the best of your ability be like me: love truth above all else; increase the awareness of all people; nurture creativity and personal evolution in yourself and others; and harm no one except to prevent them from harming yourself or others."

"So what is the difference between personal evolution and evolution in general?" I asked.

"Your species continues to evolve," said God. *"It merely obeys without choice the command I made when I started your universe. In this you have no real choice at this point. But as individuals you can choose whether you yourself continue to increase your awareness. You can read, study, meditate, explore, expand your curiosity, and delve your heart and your memories. There are infinite choices open to you. Having free will you can choose to follow my suggestion or not. You can become more godly, or not."*

"If you accept my suggestion in your personal life, you are choosing, in effect, to align your personal life with the evolution of your whole species. If enough of your kind make this choice, it will one day be known as the 'Evolutionary Ethic'. If enough humans embrace this ethic you will eventually acquire the power to command your own evolution. When you begin the conscious evolution of your species' evolution your relationship to

me will change. The transformation of your species into a being like me will have begun. Even as a child grows to adulthood, your species can grow to godhood."

"Enough! Enough!" I cried. My head was spinning with the vision He had inspired. My heart overflowed with passion. For a long time I just sat on the stony ground and sobbed; I knew not why.

"Great One, forgive me," I murmured. "I know not why I am so overcome by the vision you have given me, but I feel so inspired and at the same time so daunted by the great responsibility and many challenges that I now face. How I am to teach my people adequately all that you have revealed? How am I to persuade them to accept and embrace your wonderful 'Evolutionary Ethic'?" Again I looked down at the tablet before me.

> "God's Number One Suggestion: To the best of your ability be like me: love truth above all else; increase the awareness of all people; nurture creativity and personal evolution in yourself and others; and harm no one except to prevent them from harming yourself or others."

"You know, God, I think much of my feelings stem from my fears of being inadequate in communicating a suggestion to people who like to be commanded. Even today there are many among us who long for the days of Pharaoh's rule. As painful as it was to be slaves, it was a much simpler life; without all the responsibilities that go with freedom. I think that for my people to even begin to accept your suggestion it will be necessary to spell out what it means in a lot more detail. Would you help me with this, please."

"Of course," said God. ***"How much detail did you have in mind?"***

"You know my people, God. How much detail will they require?"

"I would suggest no more than one explanatory level containing the main logical consequences of the primary suggestion. Let them work out for themselves the rest of the details.," said God. ***"Besides, even at that it will take two tablets; and it would be best if you could carry them both in one trip down the mountain."***

"Wisdom indeed!," said I with much relief. I hadn't looked forward to the task of downloading a whole library from this high aerie.

"We'll do them one at a time," said God. ***"Do you want them labeled as explanations or as further suggestions?"***

"Can they just be Suggestion 2, Suggestion 3, ... etc.?," I asked.

"Of course," said God, ***"Here goes..."***

Again the beam of light flashed to the stone before me and as the glare eased I saw:

> "God's Number Two Suggestion: To the best of your abil-

> ity, avoid falsehood and deceit; discourage destructiveness and personal stagnation in yourself and others; and permit not harm to yourself or to others."

After I had pondered these words for a few minutes I said, "I think if I could turn your first suggestion inside out it would appear as this does."

"That's right. Do you see how it serves to amplify and explain the first suggestion?"

"Yes I do," I replied. "Let's go for number Three."

Again the flash; and then the words,

> "God's Number Three Suggestion: Think not that you can follow God's Number One Suggestion whilst ignoring God's Number Two Suggestion."

A little confused by the self-referent, I scratched my head and said, "I don't get it. What does it mean? What information is contained in the third suggestion that isn't in the second?"

"In following the Number One Suggestion you are seeking to do 'good' are you not?"

"Yes."

"And in ignoring the Number Two Suggestion you would be doing 'ill' or 'evil' wouldn't you?

"Right............. Oh, I get it. Number Three says that I can't do good deeds by evil means. As soon as I have harmed someone I have done evil, no matter who benefits by the act."

"Exactly. Here is Number Four:"

> "God's Number Four Suggestion: It is wrong to tolerate others' harmful behavior."

"And Number Five:"

> "God's Number Five Suggestion: It is wrong to do nothing; for to do so is to permit others to do harm."

"Any questions," God asked.

"No," said I, "They are quite clear. Just expansions of the First Suggestion."

"Time to start the second tablet," said God. And in another flash there was the second tablet beside the first and it read:

> "God's Number Six Suggestion: Defend yourself and others actively against injury or deceit when you or they are imminently imperiled by another's harmful behavior."

"I have a question about this one.," I said. "Just how much harm is it proper to do to someone who is trying to harm you?"

"Just enough to stop the harm they are doing."

"But what if the only way I can stop the harm results in the other person's death. Can that be right?" I asked.

"More right than permitting them to do as much to you," said God, *"when that is the alternative."*

"Does this mean," I asked, "that I and all my people should travel armed with lethal weaponry?"

"If you are committed to following my Number Six Suggestion and if there is any possibility of a potentially damaging attack on you or on those around you, that would seem to be the logical conclusion."

After a moment of thought I asked, "Does the Red Sea comprise a lethal weapon? Did I do right asking you to destroy Pharaoh's soldiers?"

"Had it been wrong I would not have done it," said God. *"After all these years are you still feeling guilty about it?"*

"I guess so," said I, "but I'd rather be struggling with my guilt feelings than long dead from not defending myself." This sixth suggestion helps. It gives me a good context for my decision to live.

"On to number seven," **said God, and with another brilliant flash these words appeared:**

> "God's Number Seven Suggestion: Withhold the augmentation of creative resources from anyone whose commitment to follow Sug-

gestions One and Two you reasonably distrust."

"Well, that makes sense," I said. "Why would I want to help someone to be destructive. If I increase their intelligence, for instance, they'll just use it to hurt me or to hurt someone else. In the end everyone would be hurt by this."

"Exactly right"; said God, ***and number eight is:***

> "God's Number Eight Suggestion: Learn new objective truths as often as possible and test new information with doubt, avoiding the seductive trap of certainty; for certainty limits your access to truth.

"Wait a minute," I interjected. "This goes contrary to most people's intuition. Surely since the dawn of time our priests, judges, and sages have always extolled the value of faith and certainty. Even Pharaoh's priesthood did so. How is it you suggest we abandon this well established tradition?"

"Moses, do you remember what I said about priests and their like? Of course they want you to have faith in what they tell you. Faith is certainty that transcends testing. They require you to be certain even when your testing proves them wrong. In their eyes the act of testing makes you a heretic. By letting them get away with such chicanery you enslave yourself to them as surely as

it would enslave you to return to Egypt and beg Pharaoh to take you back."

"But God," I moaned, "I have always told my people to have faith in *You*. What am I to tell them now?"

"I am sure, Moses, that you intended well when you asked your people to love their faith in me. But I don't need your people's faith. I am giving you something better than faith to love. Love truth instead. Not only will it serve you better, but it will force you to follow my very first suggestion, which is as I would wish."

"I'll do it; but I foresee problems convincing my people to accept that truth is better than faith. The Eldermoot, our council of spiritual advisors, will surely object."

"Of course, Moses," God rejoined, *"without your people's faith they would have little influence in your people's affairs."*

"You are certainly right about that; and I see your point. If everyone really understood your First Suggestion and all that it implies we wouldn't need spiritual advisors. The Eldermoot would be obsolete. When in doubt about the right way to apply your Suggestion to a particular situation we could just discuss it among ourselves and arrive at a good decision. In a way, it would be as though everyone would be part of the Eldermoot. Only its exclusivity would be obsolete. I like that...though I see little hope of making it a reality. So what are the last two suggestions?"

"Here they are," said God**:**

> "God's Number Nine Suggestion: When you make laws and regulations, do so only to empower the hands and hearts of those who would live by my First suggestion, and to forbid the harmful acts of those who would ignore my Second Suggestion."

"And:"

> "God's Number Ten Suggestion: When your laws and regulations are in conflict with my Suggestions, let the Suggestions prevail; your laws existing only to serve the higher purpose of the Suggestions."

"Oh, my God!" I exclaimed. "The Eldermoot is going to hate me after today. They have been making up laws like crazy; and a lot of them don't fit these criteria at all. What with taxes and campaign offerings and executive privileges and special dispensations and all...they are going to put up a great fight to discredit these last two suggestions."

"They have the distinction of being the first self-serving group to respond negatively, Moses, but I

assure you they won't be the last. Take heart. Be true. You need not fail.

"Great One," I said with a sigh, "your suggestions leave nothing to be desired. Before I return to my people I pray you tell me ought else you would have me know that will help me in the trials I am about to undertake; for surely my people's acceptance of these Suggestions will threaten the aspirations of many while they gladden the hearts of a few."

"To be sure, Moses; to be sure. Therefore, before you tell any of your people about our conversation it would be well if you related the story to the trusted scribe, Adam Kadmon, who alone among your people you can most count on to help you lay the cornerstone of the 'Evolutionary Ethic'. Require of him that he set down your story as accurately as possible in multiple copies, upon the most durable of materials available; and in the years to come to disseminate these scrolls far and wide about the earth so that the true message is never lost."

"I thank you, Great One," I said prostrating myself before the stone tablets, "God's suggestion is my command." And at these words the Burning Bush extinguished itself with the sound of a cork being drawn from the mouth of an earthen jug; and I felt God's presence withdraw. When I looked up I saw the sun was almost setting, just as it had been at the very beginning of my conversation with God. So I sat there through the night pondering all that I had learned; and in the morning I started down the mountain.

EPILOGUE BY ADAM KADMON

It has been only a moon and a day since I set down on papyrus for the first time the tale of Moses and the Ten Suggestions. Yet is seems like a year. So much has happened. So much turmoil and strife continue to result among the people.

The central point, which I believe to be worth noting, is the fact that almost overnight our citizenry has broken into conflicting factions. The one thing on which almost all seem to agree is their need to call the Suggestions by the name "Commandments". No amount of argument by Moses seems to prevail in overcoming this general objection. And while some seem to have accepted the overall admonition to "be like unto Him" contained in the First Suggestion, there are very few who don't want some special concern of theirs to be mentioned explicitly.

For instance, the members of the Eldermoot, our council of spiritual leaders, want to change the first Suggestion to tell us to revere God above all else rather than truth. Some even want it to tell us to be more *like them*, as if we need either their example or their explanation to recognize the truth. This group also wants to include an admonition to set aside a whole day each week to just listen to what *they* have to say.

Then there is the guild of craftsmen and jewelers who want the suggestions to provide some protections or special privileges for them.

And there is a contingent of disgruntled parents and grandparents who insist on including admonitions to the young to treat their elders better.

There is an emerging censorship group that wants to limit free use of the word "God". The Eldermoot is threatening to support this by demanding that only they should have the right to talk *to* God directly or *about* God generally.

Others are demanding that the so-called "Ten Commandments" should say something forbidding common crimes and sexual misbehavior; while the wealthiest group among us wants restrictions limiting aspirations of financial competition and material advantage.

As could be expected, still another group rejects the term "Evolutionary Ethic" and wants to see all reference to evolution stricken from the Commandments.

In short there seems to be no end to the efforts people will make to subvert the original message from God or to bend it to the service of their own special interests. I am appalled by the fact that so few can see in the message the foundation for the most profound personal, spiritual, social, political, and economic success imaginable. It's literally a diagram of how humans can become gods or godlike. Accordingly, I hasten to the task allotted me.

God's Ten Suggestions

"**God's Number One Suggestion: To the best of your ability be like me: love truth above all else; increase the awareness of all people; nurture creativity and personal evolution in yourself and others; and harm no one except to prevent them from harming yourself or others.**"

"**God's Number Two Suggestion: To the best of your ability, avoid falsehood and deceit; discourage destructiveness and personal stagnation in yourself and others; and permit not harm to yourself or to others.**"

"**God's Number Three Suggestion: Think not that you can follow God's Number One Suggestion whilst ignoring God's Number Two Suggestion.**"

"**God's Number Four Suggestion: It is wrong to tolerate others' harmful behavior.**"

"**God's Number Five Suggestion: It is wrong to do nothing; for to do so is to permit others to do harm.**"

"**God's Number Six Suggestion: Defend yourself and others actively against injury or deceit when you or they are imminently imperiled by another's harmful behavior.**"

"**God's Number Seven Suggestion: Withhold the augmentation of creative resources from anyone whose commitment to follow Suggestions One and Two you reasonably distrust.**"

" **God's Number Eight Suggestion: Learn new objective truths as often as possible and test new information with doubt, avoiding the seductive trap of certainty; for certainty limits your access to truth.**

" **God's Number Nine Suggestion: When you make laws and regulations, do so only to empower the hands and hearts of those who would live by my First suggestion, and to forbid the harmful acts of those who would ignore my Second Suggestion."**

" *God's Number Ten Suggestion: When your laws and regulations are in conflict with my Suggestions, let the Suggestions prevail; your laws existing only to serve the higher purpose of the Suggestions."*

CHAPTER 19

IN CONCLUSION

A plausible and credible solution to humanity's BIG PROBLEM is now in hand – or more specifically, in YOUR hands. A large ethical "business" organization can serve as the big hand on the lever – for which role it is ideally suited. The lever is the knowledge of how to eliminate hierarchies in favor of HoloMats of Octologues. The **Titania Project** is the source of the tools and knowledge that you need to learn and teach the Titanian Way. If you are as committed as I am to changing the world for the better, this is the opportunity of a lifetime. Go out and do well by doing Good!

CHAPTER 20

The Psalm Of Truth

Be true. You need not fail.
The heart of your soul is pure, strong, un
    afraid.
Your light a glowing beacon.
Passionate, eternal, unassailable.

Know truth. It cannot always elude you.
Though the minions of chaos are legion,
And their lies seductively simple;
Your laser-like mind is more than ample,
To illuminate reality, like crystalline carbon
    in the murky sea.

Imagine truly. Your other mind awaits.
The wisdom of ages past is within you,
A heartbeat away,
From the total knowledge,
Of ages yet to be.

Dream truth. As if you knew you could not
    fail.
There will never be another you;
Never another to do the things
That only you can do.
So you might as well
Be true.

APPENDICES

APPENDIX A – The Ethical Contract

There are many laws on the books that set out to define a valid contract – some are well written – others are not. The best ones contain the following basic elements and provisions:

1. The parties to the contract are clearly identified.
2. The purpose of the contract is clearly defined.
3. What each party to the contract contributes to the group participating is specified.
4. The liability that each participant undertakes – and the limitations thereto – is defined.
5. What each party to the contract is to receive in exchange for his/her participation and contribution is clearly set forth (the *quid pro quo*).
6. The duration of the agreement is specified together with the means by which the contract may be terminated.
7. The right of any participant to withdraw from the contract is affirmed; and the legal and financial consequences of such withdrawal are specified.
8. The means by which the contract can, and may be, amended are detailed.
9. Violations of the contract are defined, together with the various consequences of such violations – including various penalties to which violators may be subject.
10. The seperability of the terms of the contract is affirmed – assuring that if some portion of the contract is later deemed invalid that the remainder of the contract shall remain in effect.
11. The means by which disputes concerning the contract and other matters are to be resolved is specified.
12. The court having jurisdiction (if any) over disputes concerning the contract is specified.
13. Affirmation that each person signing the contract has read it, understands it, and has received adequate legal advice to

understand all the possible legal consequences that may result from becoming a party to it.
14. Affirmation that each person signing the contract does so of their own free will.
15. Signatures of the parties and (where applicable) signatures of witnesses.

At this point it behooves us to consider the myth of the "social contract". Many apologists for the *status quo* assert that we are all born as parties to a contract – and that, as a consequence, we are all subject to liabilities defined by the state or government. In other words, in return for the various benefits, real or imagined, that we receive from the government, we owe the government a portion of whatever resources we derive from our experience of life. We should note that the only people who promote this myth are those who want to **spend our money** or to **exercise power over us** through the enforcement of edicts forbidding *mala prohibita*. They would have us believe that they have a valid claim on the money that we receive in exchange for our creativity and productivity.

Now ask yourself:

1. Did I sign this so-called contract?
2. Did I voluntarily agree to the terms of this contract?
3. Does this contract promise to give me something that I actually want?
4. If so, am I free to acquire that which I want in other ways?
5. Does this contract contain a valid exit clause?
6. Does this contract specify the *quid pro quo* that tells me what I am to contribute and what I am to receive in return?
7. Does this contract specify what actions on the part of government constitute a breach of the contract and the penalties that attach thereto?
8. Does this contract affirm my right to withdraw from the contract?

Even proponents of this mythological contract only answer "yes" to the last question above. They say I can withdraw from the contract by giving up my citizenship and leaving the country. This is the logical equivalent of saying, "submit to the contract *or else…*" And what is the "else"? It is the loss of every birth-right that is mine – inviolate and inalienable.

Thus we see that the enforcement of this fictitious contract by edict constitutes *mala in se* – an evil (unethical) act in and of itself, unsupported even by the government's own contract laws. I categorically reject the "social contract" and defy anyone to write a cogent, rational, ethical defense of it.

So how can we *organize* a group of persons in a manner that is ethical and lawful? More specifically, how can we maximize the creativity of the group to be organized within a set of ethical constraints? The requirements of a legitimate contract, as specified above, comprise a good starting point. The mandates of the **Titanian Code of Honor** can be added because they are compatible with these contractual principles and expand somewhat the scope of the agreement upon which the group is to be organized. If properly enforced, this addition requires that the group will undertake to achieve only ethical outcomes and to use only means which are ethical ends in themselves. For a still broader set of constraints the group may choose to incorporate the **Bill of Ethics** into its founding documents or bylaws, as illustrated in the **Constitution of Titania.**

APPENDIX B: The Bill of Ethics

THE BILL OF ETHICS

By

Robert E. Podolsky

And

Gregory R. Sulliger

© 1993 by Podolsky & Sulliger

THE BILL OF ETHICS

Introduction

Robert Podolsky and Gregory Sulliger wrote the document below in 1993. It is an interpretation and extension of the work of John David Garcia as presented so thoroughly and clearly in his book, ***Creative Transformation.*** Organizations of all types can use it to amend or define their founding constitutions, charters, or by-laws. For a shorter, simpler, easier-to-remember version of this document, read ***The Titanian Code of Honor*** in APPENDIX C.

Preamble

We the undersigned officers, constituting a quorum of (Name of Organization) _____ do hereby adopt the following "Bill of Ethics" as the highest priority policy for governing all our future actions and procedures, both in our dealings with those outside our organization and in our relationships with members and/or employees within our ranks. Henceforth all other written and unwritten rules of conduct for persons associated with this organization shall be understood, reinterpreted, or if need be revised to conform to the definitions and principles stated herein.

ARTICLE 1: PHILOSOPHY & RATIONALE
- 1.1 WHEREAS this organization exists for the pursuit of ethical purposes by ethical means;
- 1.2 WHEREAS the charter of this organization establishes the right of its officers to alter and reform governing policies as they may think proper; and
- 1.3 WHEREAS the officers and members and of this organization have expressed their belief that the establishment of a Bill of Ethics would substantially promote the rights

and well-being of all who come in contact with this organization;
- 1.4 THEREFORE the policy of this organization is hereby amended, this document being appended thereto.

ARTICLE 2: DEFINITIONS
- 2.1 We believe it to be self evident that people are neither "good" nor "evil" except as their acts are "good" or "evil" ;
- 2.2 And that a person's actions are "good" (or equivalently "just" or "ethical") if they increase the creativity of at least one person, including the person acting, without limiting or diminishing the creativity of any person, including the person acting.
- 2.3 Since creativity is the product of ethical awareness and intelligence (as symbolized by the equation: $C = EI$) there are two ways an act may increase creativity.
- 2.3.1 An act may increase creativity by increasing someone's ethical awareness, degree of personal evolution, love, and/or growth, these creativity enhancers being logical equivalents of one another, in that any act which increases one of them must necessarily increase the others, and vice-versa;
- 2.3.2 An act may increase creativity by increasing the intelligence of any person who uses their intelligence creatively rather than destructively; where access to objective truth, access to energy, and freedom are enhancers of intelligence, since they increase one's ability to predict and control the environment or to initiate and maintain causal relationships between events in the observable world.
- 2.4 The lists of equivalent creativity enhancers given above are incomplete. There may in fact be an unlimited number of such equivalencies that apply. Hereinafter we shall use the words, "ethical awareness" to include all of its logical equivalents, and the word "intelligence" to similarly encompass all of its logical equivalents. The word "creativity"

- will be used to encompass both the preceding sets of resources, the distinctions between the two sets being duly noted.
- 2.5 From the preceding it follows logically that it is ethical to limit or reduce a person's intelligence in order to stop or prevent that person from acting destructively (unethically). This is generally accomplished ethically by limiting or reducing that individual's access to intelligence enhancers.
- 2.6 Where by "person" is meant any being having awareness of its own awareness... thus excluding those lower forms of life whose actions are merely "natural";
- 2.7 And acts which limit or reduce another person's creativity (or any of the equivalent resources listed in Section 2.2 above) are... with the exception explained in Section 2.5 above ...generally "bad", or equivalently "evil", "unethical", or "entropic";
- 2.8 And further, that good and evil acts by aware beings fall on an ethical continuum... where the best (most ethical) acts are those which contribute the most to the evolution of an individual or a group... and the worst (most unethical) are those which most increase the entropy (chaos or disorder) thereof;
- 2.9 And still further, that acts which are not "ethical" according to Section 2.2 above and which are not "unethical" according to Section 2.7 above may be said to be "ethically neutral", "innocent", "trivial", or merely "natural".

ARTICLE 3: PRINCIPLES
- 3.01 From the foregoing self-evident truths we infer that to act ethically each person must do his/her utmost to maximize creativity and its equivalents;
- 3.02 That ethical actions always increase someone's creativity;
- 3.03 And that ethical actions never destroy, limit, or diminish anyone's creativity except as described in Section 2.5 above.

- 3.04 And from the foregoing we infer that unethical means can never achieve ethical ends... this principle rejecting the notion that we can ethically sacrifice the creativity of the individual for the "greater good" of society, the "many", and so forth; from which it follows that:
- 3.05 Unethical means always produce unethical results (ends); trivial means always produce trivial results at best; and similarly
- 3.06 Means which are not ethical ends in themselves are never ethical;
- 3.07 From the foregoing it is also apparent that inaction is unethical. Creativity cannot be passively expanded or increased... this must be done actively to overcome entropic destruction inherent in the Second Law of Thermodynamics. This principle is basically equivalent to the adage that, "For evil to triumph it is only necessary for good men to do nothing.";
- 3.08 It also follows that it is unethical to tolerate unethical behavior. To do so is to violate Section 3.07 above. For this reason we are ethically bound to defend ourselves and others actively against injury or deceit when we or they are imminently imperiled by another's unethical behavior; from which:
- 3.08.1 It follows that it is unethical to augment the creativity of anyone whom one reasonably believes will use such augmented resources unethically... and it is therefore ethical to withhold the augmentation of creative resources from anyone whose ethical commitment one reasonably distrusts; and furthermore:
- 3.09 It is ethical to learn and unethical to be certain. When we close our minds on a subject we cease to learn... to increase our own awareness and creativity. Learning always increases creativity; and
- 3.10 It is ethical to doubt. Ceasing to have doubts about a subject we become certain about it and have ceased to

learn. Doubts create new questions ...some of which yield new answers. Doubt is one of the cornerstones of creativity.

ARTICLE 4: LAWS, RULES AND REGULATIONS

- 4.1 Be it understood that the proper role of an organization's laws, rules and regulations is to empower those people acting singly or in concert who would embrace the foregoing DEFINITIONS and PRINCIPLES set forth in Articles 2 and 3 above and who are willing to make the moral commitment to live their lives as ethically as they can... as suggested by Section 3.01.;
- 4.2 And it is also the proper role of laws, rules and regulations to prohibit by the most ethical means possible any actions which are unethical as defined above;
- 4.3 Nor is it ever the proper role of rules and regulations to intrude, coerce, or interfere, in the lives of any people except as is truly necessary in order to accomplish the aims of Sections 4.1 and 4.2 above ...such intrusion even then to be that which is minimally required;
- 4.4 Moreover, whenever the laws, rules and regulations of an organization are in conflict with said DEFINITIONS and PRINCIPLES the ethics shall prevail ...the rules being deemed to exist solely as the servant of the ETHICS, the latter being always superior to the rules.
- 4.5 RESPONSIBILITY for actions: Under the aegis of ethical rules and regulations:
- 4.5.1 All people are responsible for their own actions and the consequences which result from those actions. In determining who shall bear the burden of financial or other costs when someone's actions result in harm to another person, ultimate (though not sole or total) responsibility rests with the individual who had the last available opportunity to prevent such undesirable effects from occurring.
- 4.5.2 Also, responsibility under ethical rules is not mitigated by the failure of an individual to understand, comprehend, rationalize, or anticipate the consequences of his or

- her acts... except as such failure may alter the availability of opportunities to prevent harm from occurring.
- 4.5.3 In any case, persons who enact harm on others in a self-induced state of mental incompetence (e.g. intoxicated) may still be required to bear the costs of the consequences of their actions when the act of inducing such incompetence was the chronologically last opportunity anyone had to prevent the unethical act from being performed.
- 4.5.4 Harm enacted by one person on another is solely justifiable when necessary in self or another's defense against the person harmed.

ARTICLE 5: COOPERATION OF OFFICIALS

- **5.1 NON-INTERFERENCE:** No elected or appointed Official, officer, or employee shall take direct or indirect action or exert direct or indirect influence which would result in the circumvention, deflection, abrogation, evasion of or interference with the purpose of this policy amendment.
- **5.2 PENALTY:** Any person found to be violating Section 5.1 above shall be reprimanded or removed from their position office or appointment as determined by the authority cited below.
- **5.3 JURISDICTION:** Jurisdiction for purposes of this policy amendment, shall be with a HoloMatic Grand Jury to be chosen by the mutual consent of all parties concerned in the conflict to be adjudicated.

ARTICLE 6: PREVIOUSLY EXISTING RULES AND POLICIES

- **6.1 CONFORMITY:** Henceforth all the rules, regulations, and policies of this organization, whether they originate at board, executive, managerial, supervisory level or below shall be brought into compliance with this amendment within (time period)_____ of this date. Wherever this amendment conflicts with or contradicts other rules, regulations, or policies, be they written or unwritten, this measure shall supersede and take precedence over the other, it being the ultimate touchstone for valid procedural regulation throughout this organization.

Officers' Signatures: Date:

_____   _____

_____   _____

_____   _____

© 1993 by Podolsky and Sulliger

Revised 10/15/2014

APPENDIX C
The Titanian Code of Honor

The TITANIAN CODE OF HONOR, is a set of four simple affirmations containing the most prominent logical consequences of the Titanian Ethic. These affirmations and a brief explanation of each are shown below. If you decide to join Titania, in any capacity, you will be expected to honor this code.

A) **We do no harm.**
B) **We do good at every opportunity.**
C) **The CODE always applies – no exceptions**
D) **Everyone knows the CODE.**

EXPLANATIONS

A. **DEFINITIONS**

1. An act is good if it increases creativity, or any of its logical equivalents, for at least one person, including the person acting, without limiting or diminishing creativity for anyone.

2. Logical equivalents of creativity include: love, awareness, personal evolution, the availability of objectively true information to ethical persons, and possibly many other resources.

3. A second set of creativity-enhancing resources are sometimes necessary, often helpful, and never sufficient, for the maximization of creativity; however they are not logical equivalents of creativity and their maximization in lieu of creativity can result in unethical outcomes. These resources include, but are not limited to: freedom, privacy,

honesty, empathy, conscience, energy, wealth, profit, and even happiness.

The explanations that follow are simply logical consequences of the above definitions.

B. WE DO NO "HARM"

1. We never attempt to achieve ethical ends by unethical means.

2. We never lie - except in self-defense, in which case lying may be mandatory.

3. We never coerce – except in self-defense.

4. We never steal, destroy, limit, or diminish anyone's physical, tangible, mental, intellectual, temporal, or emotional resources.

5. We never invade another's privacy.

6. We never excuse our own ethical lapses.

7. We never destroy, limit, or avoid corrective feedback.

8. We never attempt to delegate authority that we do not possess as individuals.

9. We never employ "majority rule".

10. We never perform (act) as a group in a way that would be unethical if performed by an individual.

11. We never support, nurture, or augment the abilities of anyone whose actions are predatory, parasitic, or

generally unethical. Nor do we permit such acts when presented with a choice in the matter.

12. We never obey rules/edicts that forbid ethical behavior or require unethical behavior.

B. **WE CONSISTENTLY DO "GOOD"**

1. We always seek to maximize creativity, love, awareness, personal evolution, and their logical equivalents above all else and at every opportunity.

2. We commit to those actions which fulfill this mission.

3. We commit to using only those means which are ethical ends in themselves.

4. At every opportunity we help and augment the freedom, independence, autonomy, privacy, knowledge, courage, and other creativity-enhancing resources of those whom we trust to act in accordance with the CODE.

5. We ask for and accept the help of others.

6. We ask for and accept the corrective feedback available from others.

7. We offer our own corrective feedback to others, especially where ethical decision-making is concerned.

8. We augment one another's strengths and compensate for one another's weaknesses.

9. We maintain security and confidentiality.

10. We celebrate all individual and group success.

11. We share expenses and profits as agreed.

12. We are paid for our creativity and productivity – not for our time.

C. **THE CODE APPLIES AT ALL TIMES – NOT JUST WHEN IT IS EASY OR CONVENIENT.**

D. **EVERYONE KNOWS THE CODE** – Now you do too.

APPENDIX D

ETHICAL MEANS AND ETHICAL ENDS
Excerpted from *"BORG WARS"*
By

Robert E. Podolsky

I distinguish here four categories of unethical acts and note that the most harmful in our society are those in which the decision to act unethically is the result of ignorance or misunderstanding concerning basic ethical principles. In particular I examine the most harmful and widespread fallacy that ethical ends can be attained by unethical means. This simple mistaken notion is arguably the single greatest source of evil in the world today. If this fact were generally understood the world of humanity would be a far better place in which to live.

Types of "Sins"
At any given time a person wishing to act ethically must choose a particular action over other possibilities knowing that the information on which the decision to act is based is incomplete. Therefore the individual making the choice must estimate the probabilities of various consequences that are foreseen as possible results of the choices available knowing that unimagined consequences are possible and that yet-to-be-imagined choices may exist with still more unforeseen consequences. Sometimes the moral individual makes these choices in full awareness of their personal limitations and sometimes not. But no one can know with certainty all the outcomes of their acts, not even after the action has taken place.

For the reasons given above, we all make mistakes in choosing our actions; and sometimes our actions, made in moral good faith, have results that we deem unethical. Knowing this is humbling to us all. When it happens we say, "Oh, if only I had known; I would have acted differently". For lack of a better name, let me call these unintended lapses "Type One Sins" or T-1s for short. Such moral lapses are literally unavoidable no matter how committed we are to acting as ethically as possible. They are made with the least possible awareness that the outcome will be unethical.

Now let us consider unethical acts undertaken with more awareness on the part of the one acting that the action will have destructive results. At the other end of the spectrum from the T-1s are actions that are taken knowing full well that they are hurtful and destructive; yet they are taken nonetheless; the actor often *enjoying* the knowledge that someone is being hurt. Such actions are sadistic at best and unmitigatedly *evil* in their more extreme manifestations. Let us call such actions "Type Four Sins" or T-4s for short.

Enacted in the absence of malice are those hurtful actions taken with regret on the part of the one acting; believing that circumstances render it the most ethical choice available. For instance, consider the medic who administers an emergency tracheotomy to save the life of a person choking to death in spite of the fact that there is some pain inflicted in the process. The medic takes no pleasure in the infliction of this pain; recognizes that the infliction of pain is unethical and does so anyway seeing no other way to save the patient's life. Let us call unethical acts of this variety "Type Three Sins" or T-3s for short.

And finally I come to the subject of this article; namely those moral lapses that result in unethical outcomes because the person acting lacks a fundamental understanding of ethics. This category, which I shall call "Type Two Sins" or T-2s for short, is, as we shall see, the most serious challenge on the planet to humanity's long-range survival. How so? Consider the following.

T-1s are unavoidable; but are never carried out systematically and are never institutionalized.

T-4s are only committed by psychopaths, sociopaths, and other persons who are devoid of conscience. Such people are in a very small minority, are easily identified, and are rarely tolerated in human society, the majority finding their way into our "corrections" systems at a fairly early age – though a successful minority become lawyers, politicians, or corporate CEOs.

T-3s are usually mitigated in their harmfulness by the thoughtfulness and reluctance of the person acting.

But T-2s are another story altogether. As we shall see, their destructive scope can be systemic; they have the potential to make humanity extinct; and, what is more, they are often institutionalized by governments, businesses, religions, and other powerful interest groups whose resources make them far more destructive than T-1s, T-3s, and T4s together.

Defining the Good Act
Most of us have no problem understanding that an act or behavior that benefits someone and harms no one is clearly ethical. Similarly we understand intuitively that an act or behavior that harms someone and benefits no one is clearly unethical. Our difficulties with ethical concepts begin when we contemplate an act or behavior that has both beneficial and harmful consequences. So, for purposes of the present discussion, consider the following two definitions as candidates for the foundation of a system of ethics.

1. An ethical act is one that benefits at least one person (even if only the person acting) while harming no one (including the person acting).

2. An ethical act is one that causes more benefits to people than it does harm.

For the present I put aside the task of defining what constitutes a "benefit" or "harm". That part is comparatively easy. Just assume for the moment that adequate definitions of these terms are in fact available. The hard part is the choice between the two definitions. The first definition asserts that to be ethical an act must harm no one; and that therefore an act that harms someone is unethical.

This definition therefore forbids the achievement of ethical ends by unethical means.

The second definition, however, allows the use of unethical (harmful) means if the act does more benefit than harm. Let's assume for the moment that it is possible to quantify benefits and harms (this can in fact be done) and notice that this definition would lead us to believe that ethical ends can be achieved by unethical means. This has in fact been the ethic, which most human societies have adopted. Opinion to the contrary notwithstanding, this is the preferred choice of governments, corporations, and religious institutions worldwide. It is ***historically*** what we have actually done.

As similar as these definitions seem, the outcomes produced by the choice of one or the other are as different as night and day. ***One choice leads to the maximization of peace, love, and prosperity and the other leads to wars, genocide, poverty, cruelty, exploitation and slavery***. There are at least three distinct and essentially independent proofs of the preceding assertion. I call these the **"Historical Proof"**, the **"Golden Rule Proof"**, and the **"Logical Proof"**. These are presented in the following.

THE HISTORICAL PROOF

Values and Beliefs

To help understand the distinction between the two definitions of a good act and its significance I review the concepts of values and beliefs. I have personally interviewed over a thousand people asking questions about what they want more of in life; what they really value. The similarity between people's answers is pretty amazing. Health, basic comforts, spiritual peace of mind, love, freedom, mobility, good relationships and time to enjoy them; access to truth; mental stimulation, work that feels meaningful, growth stimuli, pleasure, happiness, and opportunities to enhance the lives of others are among those frequently mentioned. It is not hard for most of us to agree on what is "good"; what we value. In this respect humanity is pretty homogeneous. We have little disagreement about our basic values.

Far more difficult it is to reach any kind of agreement on what will actually bring us what we value. What we believe is needed in order to attain what we want we refer to as our individual belief system. All living things have values and belief systems. Even a plant that has just enough awareness to *value* sunlight may turn its leaves perpendicular to the rays of the sun in the *belief* that this will increase its access to that which it values.

When it comes to belief systems we tend to lose our objectivity; to trust faith over truth even though reality consistently demonstrates the fact that objective truth is repeatable, verifiable, and pragmatically irrefutable. In other words we tend to believe what we want to believe even if our collective experience contradicts us.

Let's go back to the example of the plant that turns its leaves perpendicular to the rays of the sun. In situations where plants compete for sunlight those that have this awareness, belief, and ability enjoy a competitive advantage. Other things being equal, they *do* get more sun than their less phototropic counterparts. This fact has been thoroughly established by many experiments by many different experimenters using a wide range of techniques. So in the plant's case the belief that phototropism maximizes sunlight reception is correct. One might say that plants that believe otherwise are wrong and that many of them suffer for lack of the correct belief. In fact, some have probably become extinct for lack of the correct belief.

Similarly when we choose the basic definition of our ethics, that which we define as a good act, we may or may not choose correctly that which will optimize our chances of getting what we most value in life. If we choose incorrectly, we too may become extinct for lack of the correct belief system. In this way we can compare the values of various belief systems. Definitions, like other statements, are composed of information that can either be "true" or "false". True information is that which when believed increases the intelligence of the believer. "Intelligence" in this context is the ability to predict and control events in the observable universe, or equivalently to initiate and sustain causal relationships between such events. This definition of true information is the basis of science and in many ways can be seen as defining science. That is to say, any discipline that uses this definition of truth may be said to be a science.

Now let's review the two definitions stated previously which I from now on refer to as **E1** (Ethic 1) and **E2** (Ethic 2) respectively:

1. An ethical act is one that benefits at least one person (even if only the person acting) while harming no one (including the person acting).

2. An ethical act is one that causes more benefits to people than it does harm.

These two definitions are similar in that both value "benefits" while seeking to avoid "harms". But each of these definitions, when accepted, yields a dramatically different belief system. In other words while sharing the fundamental values inherent in each definition, people adopting one or the other of these definitions as the basis for their behavior will behave very differently.

As in the case of plant phototropism, there have been enough "experiments" with these two definitions for us to know how individuals and groups develop when one or the other of these two ethics is adopted. One of these definitions is "true" and yields a belief system that maximizes the intelligence of the believer; and the other is "false" because it substantially diminishes the intelligence of its believer.

The true definition is the first: "An ethical act is one that benefits at least one person (even if only the person acting) while harming no one (including the person acting)." Individuals and groups adopting this definition are universally better off than those who don't. We'll have more to say about this later.

The second definition turns out to be one of humanity's greatest stumbling blocks. It often seduces us into forgetting that the choice of the "lesser evil" is still a choice of evil. Governments, corporations, and religious bureaucracies throughout the world have long given in to the temptation to adopt this definition and the belief systems that result from its adoption.

The unacknowledged prioritization of the desires for power, money, and self-righteousness lead the adopters of this definition to think that if **they** benefit from their decisions, that harm done to **others** is acceptable. It is easy for such people to see that **they** benefit more than they are harmed by this ethic (at least on a short-term basis); and therefore not so easy to see that the ethic itself is flawed and that it causes them and others enormous harm on a long-term basis.

Let's examine some of the historical consequences of this false belief system. One common theme that results from the adoption and institutionalization of **E2** is the idea that the well being of some people (sometimes referred to as "the few") must be sacrificed for the well being of others (sometimes called "the many"). Hence:

- All instances of slavery throughout history are based on this premise, resulting in the suffering and annihilation of millions of people.
- Religions that condoned or required human sacrifice were based on this premise; which is part of the reason that most such religions are essentially extinct today – though I'm told a few are still with us.
- Marxist-Leninist regimes have always been based on this premise, resulting in near-universal poverty for those living in such countries.
- The government practice of taxation is based on this belief, resulting in the financial enslavement of billions of people today. I would go so far as to assert (Podolsky's theorem) that every time a government seeks to solve a societal problem by levying a tax that in the long run the society is harmed far more than it benefits.

- The rise of corporate power and its concomitant partnership with government is the result of this belief; and results in the disenfranchisement of billions of people worldwide.
- The power-ascendancy of religious organizations is the result of this misconception, and has been the basis of pogroms, jihads, crusades, holy wars, inquisitions and similar large-scale atrocities for thousands of years.
- Many activities seen as normal components of war are based on this idea; not the least of which is the concept that civilian casualties are an acceptable price to pay to win a war.

These are just a few examples of institutionalized T-2 sins as I have defined them here. Each and every one of them has at one time or another been justified by adoption of **E2** as the prevailing ethic. This historical perspective tells us that these evils occur in spite of our wish to cause more good than harm; and in fact happen in large measure *because* we chose to define a good or ethical act as one that creates more benefits than harms *without placing a limit on the amount of harm that is permissible*. How can this be?

To answer this question let's go back and take a closer look at the consequences of Ethics Definition Number 1. It states: An ethical act is one that benefits at least one person (even if only the person acting) while harming no one (including the person acting). Note that this definition logically implies that any act that is harmful to someone is unethical...by definition. Acceptance of this definition precludes all the harmful consequences listed above as resulting from Definition 2. It means it is not acceptable to sacrifice the one for the benefit of the many. It is not acceptable to take away people's resources by force no matter who benefits; so only voluntary "taxes" are ethical and Marx's redistribution of wealth is unethical. Control of government by institutions that place a highest value on power or profits is unethical; so public disempowerment by corporations and organized religions is necessarily unacceptable. And of course, warfare that harms non-combatants is also unethical, as are business practices that degrade the environment.

To put it bluntly, our society is in a mess today because we don't have an institutionalized understanding that ethical ends ***cannot*** be achieved by unethical means. If our institutions incorporated this awareness and committed themselves to Ethics Definition 1 (**E1**) all the aforesaid T-2 sins would be abolished and a far more successful society would have a chance to evolve. This is the most important issue that humanity faces today; yet here in the United States, one of the most successful and enlightened countries in the world, we don't address this issue publicly; our presidential candidates give no hint of being aware of it; and the media for all their investigative expertise are oblivious to it.

At this point I have one unfinished item to deal with. How are we to recognize "benefits" and "harms"? The best definition I have seen is that an act is beneficial if it increases someone's creativity ***or any of its logical equivalents***. A resource is a logical equivalent of creativity if the increase or decrease of that resource necessitates a corresponding increase or decrease in creativity and *vice versa*. Some examples of creativity's logical equivalents are awareness, love, objective truth, personal growth, and evolution. Similarly, an act is harmful if it limits or diminishes creativity or any of its logical equivalents for anyone.

It should also be noted that creativity might be thought of as the product of ethical awareness and intelligence as symbolized by the equation $C=EI$, where C can be positive or negative; and negative creativity is the equivalent of destructiveness or entropy maximization. In this sense "evolution" and "entropy" are logical equivalents of "good" and "evil" respectively.

In the first paragraph of this chapter I said that the single greatest source of evil in the world today is the idea that ethical ends can be achieved by unethical means. Subsequently I have shown that this mistaken notion historically generates unethical deeds of the T-2 variety and that such misdeeds are widely institutionalized and wreak great harm on all humanity.

One of these Type Two sins I have not yet mentioned; and it is arguably the most destructive. It is called "bureaucracy". "Bureaucracy" is often thought to be a synonym for "organization"; but it is not. It is not even a logical equivalent of organization. As John David Garcia first pointed out to me, bureaucracy is the systematic elimination of corrective feedback; and at its worst is the elimination of feedback concerning ethics.

It is this phenomenon that brought down the Soviet Union and the Roman Empire and many other regimes throughout history. It is gradually destroying the United States and its allies even now. Unless we reverse this entropy-increasing trend we too will go the way of earlier fallen regimes and quite possibly we may destroy all humanity in the process.

When employees the world over can go to their "superiors" and criticize their employers' ethics without fear of reprisals, bureaucracy will no longer be a major problem for humanity. When those same employees can reveal their challenges to those same "superiors" and receive helpful feedback that makes them better at their jobs we will have little to fear from the depredations of bureaucracy. Until that day the insistence by so many that ethical ends can be achieved by unethical means will continue to eat away at our species' potential. Which force will dominate our lives in this new century; evolution or entropy?

THE "GOLDEN RULE PROOF"

Many people claim to live by the Golden Rule: "***Do unto others as you would have them do unto you***". But I shall prove now that choosing **E2** as one's operative ethic is in contradiction to the Golden Rule.

One obvious implication of the Golden Rule is the admonition, "***Do not do unto others as you would not have them do unto you.***" This is a corollary of the Golden Rule, as it follows from it by logic alone. Of course both admonitions could be contained in one by stating the rule: ***"Do unto others only as you would have them do unto you."***

Now consider what happens when one takes an action that is constrained only by the **E2** ethic. In general such an action has consequences that produce both beneficial and harmful effects where the harms are constrained to be less than the benefits. In some instances the benefits and harms will be sustained by the same individual; but in general the benefits and harms are permitted to apply to separate people, whereby one or more persons are benefited and one or more are harmed.

Now I ask, "Did the people harmed volunteer to be harmed? Did we do unto them as we would have them do unto us?" In all honesty we can only answer "NO, OF COURSE NOT" to these questions. Therefore the **E2** ethic is an insufficient constraint to prevent its adherents from ***doing unto others as they would NOT have others do unto themselves***. The **E2** ethic therefore unequivocally violates the Golden Rule and should be unacceptable to anyone who esteems the Golden Rule as their highest ethic.

THE LOGICAL PROOF

In this section I shall prove by logic alone that the **E2** ethic is unacceptable if we are ever to have universal peace and prosperity. I do this because some of us do not give any special credence to ethics such as the Golden Rule because it derives from biblical lore. No matter. We can show in effect that the **E2** ethic contains its own contradiction; that an act sanctioned by **E2** must be unethical if it is not also sanctioned by **E1.**

To understand this proof one must first consider the fact that in general an act sanctioned by **E2,** unless also sanctioned by **E1,** will have as consequences both beneficial and harmful effects. Observing those effects we recognize a principle of seperability: ***An act or behavior, which has both beneficial and harmful effects, is logically and ethically indistinguishable from two acts, one having beneficial consequences and the other having harmful con-***

sequences. This fact is apparent when you consider that after the consequences have been manifested you cannot tell whether the cause of those consequences was one act or two.

Now I go back to an earlier statement. An act that has only beneficial consequences is clearly ethical; and an act that has only harmful consequence is clearly unethical. From this we deduce that in general an **E2** sanctioned behavior is the logical and ethical equivalent of two acts, one of which is ethical and the other unethical. But a behavior cannot be both ethical and unethical. Any behavior that encompasses an unethical act must be unethical. Therefore I conclude that any act sanctioned by **E2** that is not also sanctioned by **E1** must be unethical. Therefore adoption of **E2** must lead to unethical behavior. This is how the institutionalization of **E2** causes so many serious societal problems (T-2 sins). If we have any hope of success as a species, humanity must come to grips with this issue by institutionalizing **E1** in place of **E2**.

SUMMARY

The choice of an ethic determines the quality of the values and belief systems that derive there from. As we have seen, the ethical definition that leads to a healthier society is the **E1** ethic that defines an ethical act as one that benefits someone without harming anyone. I believe I have proven unequivocally that adoption of the **E2** ethic (which defines as ethical any act that results in more benefit than harm) must lead to unethical outcomes; and in particular has led to wholesale evils through the attempt to achieve ethical ends by unethical means.

The "Historical Proof" shows that human experience is a clear demonstration of the failure of **E2** to limit the harms done in the name of benefits for the many.

The "Golden Rule Proof" validates this empirical observation by showing that the **E2** ethic violates the Golden Rule. And finally the "Logical Proof" shows that **E2** contains its own contradiction; so that any institution defining its ethics by adoption of **E2** is likely to create more harms than benefits in spite of its intention to do otherwise.

APPENDIX E
WHY TAXATION IS SLAVERY

I have maintained for some time that taxation is government's most criminal enterprise and that it is, in fact, a form of slavery. Yet it continues to baffle me that so many people cannot or will not see the obvious truth in these statements and insist on arguing that taxation is necessary to humanity's well being and that it is not slavery at all.

"The greatest good for the greatest number" goes the usual utilitarian (**E2**) refrain...which I maintain is one of the greater falsehoods...for the usual reasons. But since these reasons are so elusive to the greatest number I have decided to explain my reasoning in language that (hopefully) anyone can understand, thus settling this dispute once and for all in the eyes of any reasonable person.

While a whole book might easily be devoted to this subject, it is my intention to present here only a brief treatise on the subject in order to make the information as accessible as possible. I present herein three separate, but not entirely independent, arguments to make my case. I call them respectively:

1. The Property Rights Argument,
2. The Robin Hood Argument, and
3. The Smart Business Argument.

The Property Rights Argument is the one usually presented by libertarians in the manner of the late Murray Rothbard. Unfortunately, Rothbard presupposed that most people would accept intuitively that people own their own bodies. From this assumption he then reasoned that this implied the existence of property rights and hence absolute ownership of whatever the individual might create or produce. While the reasoning behind this argument is correct, few people accept it because it is counter-intuitive. It is counter-intuitive because as children it is obvious to us that our parents own our bodies, rather than we ourselves. When we go to school our teachers appear to own us. And when we grow up and become employees, it often seems that our employers own us. We also observe as adults that if we refuse to pay taxes we can involuntarily lose possession of all our assets, thus demonstrating that government has a higher claim than we do to whatever we would like to believe we own. In the midst of such a society it is hardly surprising that most of us are unconvinced that we have any property rights not mitigated by government decree.

So it follows that if indeed we have any property rights worth discussing we will need some other way to discover this fact than simply agreeing with the Rothbard assertion that we own our own bodies. Fortunately there is another avenue of reasoning that we can call upon for this purpose. It begins with the definition of an ethical act:

> **An act is ethical if it increases the creativity of anyone, including the person acting, without limiting or diminishing the creativity of anyone.**

As I have shown elsewhere, this definition is logically equivalent to similar definitions in which the word "creativity" is replaced by "love", "awareness", "personal evolution", or any of a potentially large set of resources that are logical equivalents of creativity. I have also conclusively shown, in the preceding appendix, that the utilitarian definition defining an ethical act as one that does more good than harm is invalid, and that because of this that it follows by simple logic that ethical ends cannot ever be attained by unethical means no matter who (or how many) benefits from such an act.

Now let's ask the question, "Might it be ethical to steal someone's possessions, either by force or by deceit?" And the answer is a resounding, "NO!" The scientist depends on her computer. The poet depends on his word processor. The artist needs her brushes and paints. Steal these things from someone and they are rendered less creative. By definition such an act is unethical…bad…evil. It follows logically from this that if we have the "right" to be treated ethically then we must have the "right" to own whatever we are able to acquire without stealing from someone else…and that therefore no one has the right, for any reason, to deprive us of the fruit of our bodies' labor.

By similar reasoning it follows that we do indeed own our own bodies and that any act which abrogates that right of ownership is an act of slavery because it diminishes our self-ownership. If our physical and financial possessions indeed contribute to our creativity, then it follows that the systematic removal of any such resources from our possession is evil and is a form of enslavement. Taxation is just such an act.

The Robin Hood Argument is even easier to understand. We begin the discussion with my asking you the question, "Would it be all right with you if I stole your assets?"

And of course your answer is, "No."

Next I ask, "Would it matter to you whether the theft was by force or by fraud?"

Again you answer, "No."

Then I ask, "Would you care what I did with the money?"

Again, "No."

Then I ask, "What if I gave the money away…would that make it okay?"

Again, "No."

"Suppose I gave half the money to a lot of poor people and they liked it and wanted more. Would that make the theft okay with you?"

Still, "No."

"Suppose all those poor folks elected a bunch of congressmen and I gave the other half of your money to them to spend as they wished. Would that make the theft okay with you?"

Still, "No."

"Finally, suppose those congressmen got together and wrote a piece of paper saying it was all right for me to steal from you and give away the proceeds; and they called that piece of paper a 'tax law'. Would that make the theft okay with you?"

At this point I hope you have the good sense to continue saying, "No. NO. NO!"

Now I put it to you that the above description is exactly the reality that you face in relation to government as we know it today. The "I" in the example above is the IRS. It takes away your money by means of coercion, intimidation, and force and gives it to others who claim to legitimize the theft on the basis of majority rule, public benefit, wealth distribution, homeland security, etc., etc., etc. To the extent that the above description is correct, the government is a thieving parasite and you are its host. To the extent that you don't get to keep the fruit of your labor the government owns it, not you; and to that extent you are a slave.

I should say a few words here about *how* the government steals from you. It does so in three ways. First it taxes you **directly** by means of income taxes, property taxes, sales taxes, parking and traffic tickets, court imposed fines, school and utility district assessments, licensing and registration fees, gasoline, alcohol, and tobacco taxes, etc.

Then there are taxes passed on to you indirectly. Most of these are taxes paid by the businesses which make or import the things you buy. Every time the government requires a tariff for the importation of foreign goods or raw materials it requires you to pay more and get less. If your *Toyota* dealer pays a tariff, then you are paying more for a car than the free market would charge. If you save yourself the added expense by buying a *Ford*, then in effect your government insists you settle for an inferior product so that *Ford* can make a bigger profit. This amounts to an **indirect** tax. Either way value is taken away from you and given to someone else who didn't earn it.

And finally there are hidden taxes. The most blatant example of a hidden tax is inflation...the illusion of rising prices. Every time the Federal Reserve prints money for the government to spend, the government gets the full value of each Federal Reserve "dollar" printed. But shortly after the money is spent by the government it is absorbed by the economy and the value of every dollar in your bank account is diminished. In effect the government thereby steals the buying power of all of your money without your even knowing that you are being taxed[7]. Since the passage of the Federal Reserve Act in 1913, the dollar has lost at least 96% of its buying power in this way – and possibly as much as 99.3%.

All in all, if one includes direct, indirect, and hidden taxes, the average American gives up 50% or more of their gross income to local, state, and federal authorities by way of taxes – though, again, some estimates run much higher. That means that at least half the fruit of your labor is forfeit whether you like it or not. Is it any less odious to be a half time slave than it would be to live as a full time slave? I think not? Slavery is slavery.

The Smart Business Argument starts with a fantasy. Imagine I am a slave owner and you are one of my hard-working slaves whom I use as labor in my agricultural business. They (and you) plant my fields and harvest my crops, which I sell at a substantial profit. My business depends on them. While you may think that

---

[7] See ***The Creature from Jekyll Island, a Second Look at the Federal Reserve System*** by G. Edward Griffin,

slave labor is free to me, the fact is that it is not. Besides the initial purchase of my slaves, I have to maintain them. I feed, clothe, and house them…albeit cheaply, but it's not free. I pay for whatever medical expenses I decide to invest in for their health and I pay for their management, which includes the services of bounty hunters who round them up for me when they escape.

I also have to pay for the tools and implements that my slaves use and the seeds that they plant. All in all it's an expensive operation. What is more, I am limited in the geographical scope over which I can deploy my slaves, so my business is pretty much limited to the acreage contiguous to my home. This limits my profits still further.

Not wishing to remain so limited I consult a savvy business advisor and soon create a labor cartel together with a number of my colleagues. The cartel in turn goes into partnership with the government. Soon thereafter I round up all my slaves to attend a meeting at which I make the following announcements:

"As of today your life will be different. Subject to certain rules and conditions, you and all other slaves will hereby be set free. The purpose of the rules is to reimburse me and my colleagues for the investment that we have made in you. When that debt has been paid, you will be completely free for all time. These are the rules:

1. *You can live anywhere in the world you wish. As of today you can live in any housing you can afford. You pay for your own.*

2. *You can do any kind of work you want to do. You will work whatever hours you and your employer agree upon.*

3. *You will attend school through at least the age of 18 in preparation for your work. You will pay for your schools through taxes.*

4. *You may own a business if you so desire and are able to acquire the capital needed to start it, and pay a tribute for the opportunity to make money from the efforts of others to do so.*

5. *You will carry an identification token all your life and through it your income will be tracked. I will know where you are working and for whom. I will know how much you earn and where you bank.*

6. *Directly and indirectly you will pay me and my colleagues 50¢ out of every dollar that you earn. This will apply toward payment of your debt to me.*

7. *If you need to borrow additional money and can convince a bank that you are a good 'credit risk', money will be created for you with the stroke of a computer key. This money costs the bank nothing to create and represents no risk to the bank, but if you fail to repay it with interest the bank will take away your house, your car, or any other assets you have that the bank required as collateral for the loan.*

8. *When the government needs to spend more money than it has collected in taxes, it will 'borrow' it from the Federal Reserve System which is a cartel of the world's biggest banks. It will not need your permission to do this, but you and your descendents will be responsible for repayment of the loan. It will simply be added to whatever you already owe[8]. Naturally the value (buying power) of all the money (Federal Reserve Notes) in your possession will steadily diminish as the Fed continues this practice, so of course your debt to me and my colleagues will never be repaid in full.*

---

[8] Fully one half of your direct federal taxes today go to pay the interest on such loans.

> 9. In order to maintain your sense of freedom you will participate in general elections at regular intervals. The majority vote will determine who occupy the positions of elected officialdom. But the rules above will never be changed to your advantage... only to the advantage of the banking and labor cartels that are actually the owners of the whole system (including you). Accordingly, discussion of these rules will never be part of the general debate at election time. (Meta-Meta Rules)
>
> 10. The local, state, and federal governments of the United States will be responsible for enforcement of the rules above in keeping with its partnership in the banking and labor cartels. The courts will adjudicate any conflicts that arise; but discussion of these rules will be forbidden in court and any reference to them will be deemed 'frivolous' by the courts. In this way the rules become in themselves a form of law more potent and inviolable than the state and federal constitutions and local charters that might otherwise interfere with the working of the rules."

The rules above are just "smart business" from the viewpoint of the modern slave owner. Costs are held to a minimum. Productivity is maximized. The slaves manage themselves. There are no rebellions to be concerned with. And yet the slaves are easy to manipulate and control using modern methods of scholastic indoctrination and media communication. What a blessing that most of the slaves have no inkling whatever that they *are in fact* still slaves. This fact alone makes the whole system worth whatever sacrifices the slave owners have made to create it, because there are no organized modes of resistance to the system. Even the organized religions don't protest the half-time slavery imposed on the public. What a deal for the owners of the system!

In Conclusion, I ask you not to feel too badly if you didn't get it before now...if you didn't realize that you are a slave. Most of us don't get it and billions of dollars are spent each year to keep us in the dark about it. By maintaining the illusion that we are not slaves the system's owners remain free to continue their perpetuation of the system, with the eventual (though not too distant) goal of taking over the whole world. If we don't act promptly and with vigor that goal will be attained…very probably within your lifetime. As the goal is neared the deceit will become less and less subtle and the limitations on our freedom more and more pronounced.

With the exceptions of 1865 and 1920 (emancipation and suffrage) we have had less freedom every year than the year before. This book points the way to the only viable solution that I can see to the, otherwise inevitable, outcome of global slavery and the concomitant degradation of the social and physical environments of the world…to the detriment of all…including those who will be the world's rulers. It is a universal characteristic of parasites that, in the end, they destroy their host and, with it, themselves.

Appendix F
Dr. Deming's Admonitions

Introduction

In 1950 Dr. William Edward Deming transformed the world of industry. He did this by teaching the Japanese how to succeed in making products that would outsell those of all other nations. At that time "made in Japan" meant "cheap shoddy imitation" to most people around the world. Five years later Dr. Deming's advice had made Japanese industry a force to be reckoned with in the world marketplace. Today, fifty years later, the Japanese credit Deming's advice with their clearly dominant position in the world of manufacturing. How ironic it is that American auto manufacturers had laughed at Dr. Deming when he offered to teach them the wisdom of what he called "statistical quality control".

Although revered in Japan, Dr. Deming remained little known in the U.S. until recently. Now some American industrialists are scurrying to learn and apply what he taught the Japanese in 1950. If it were not for the work of a few dedicated authors (referenced at the end of this article) Dr. Deming's work might still be unknown in the U.S. today. In the five to ten years before his death in 1993 Dr. Deming formulated an American version of his advice to the Japanese. It contains all the valuable information to which the Japanese were privy as well as some advice specific to the needs of American industry.

In this formulation, as reported in Mary Walton's excellent book, the advice consists of fourteen "points", seven "deadly diseases", and four "obstacles" for American industry to be concerned about. For convenience sake we refer to this body of knowledge collectively as Dr. Deming's twenty-five "Admonitions".

It is our contention that these Admonitions are not just a convenient set of guidelines for the improvement of industry; but rather they constitute, together with the Japanese experience in applying them, the living proof of the validity of a broader set of principles from which the Admonitions can be logically derived. This broader set of principles, which we call the **Bill of Ethics,** may have the power to do for all humankind what the Admonitions have done for Japanese industry. If this premise proves correct it could spell the difference between human extinction and the long-range success of the human species.

In the pages that follow we intend first to describe briefly the Admonitions and their significance. Then we will turn our attention to the **Bill of Ethics** and briefly talk about its origins and structure; and identify the parts of it that are directly applicable to the derivation of the Admonitions.

Next we will derive a simplified form of the admonitions that is logically equivalent to the original form, but simpler to deal with as a logical entity. Then we will set forth a reasonable credibility argument to the effect that each and every useful part of the Admonitions is demonstrably derivable from no more than six parts of the Bill of Ethics and possibly from as few as two. We find this credibility argument so compelling that we shall leave it to others to set forth a more rigorous proof thereof. Naturally, we also invite opinions to the contrary. Finally we intend to address the "So what?" concerning this derivation and discuss the reasons we think that its general acceptance could be an important turning point for humanity.

The Significance of Dr. Deming's Admonitions

Each year the Japanese government awards The Deming Prize to businesses and individuals who have made outstanding achievements in applying Dr. Deming's Admonitions. In years when no significant advances have been made no prize is awarded. The Deming Prize is arguably the most sought after award in Japan. Everyone who works in Japan knows about it and strives to receive its award. Its recipients are given the highest respect the Japanese can confer. While American students are saluting the flag, Japanese children learn to recite the Admonitions.

In part this preoccupation of the Japanese is a celebration of their success on the battlefield of commerce; a vindication, if you will, of the ignominy of their defeat in W.W.II. But more than that, it is a celebration of the day-to-day experience of working in an environment that protects, nurtures, and appreciates them. It is emotionally rewarding to work for a company that takes the admonitions seriously. Point number seven is "Institute Leadership - Help people to do a better job". Point number eight is "Drive out fear". Point number eleven is "Eliminate numerical quotas". Number twelve is "Remove barriers to pride of workmanship". The third Deadly Disease is merit ratings and annual performance reviews. The Japanese have eliminated them.

In the resulting environment workers experience a bond with the company and work as if they owned it. This includes making numerous suggestions for improvement of every feature of the work experience. Experimentation is commonplace in this environment because workers and managers are not afraid to make mistakes in their joint search for a better way. They become partners rather than adversaries.

If American unions really cared about the well-being of their members they would demand that the workplace be "Deming-ized". If they got their way the unions would have to disband because their adversarial stance would be a barrier to the effective application of the Admonitions. Japanese factories in the United States are run in this same way. They are never unionized. Who needs a union to speak for them when they can speak for themselves and be heard by sympathetic ears?

The Demingized work environment, also known as the Total Quality work environment, is a joy to be a part of compared with traditional authoritarian workplaces. Workers in this setting generally feel valued, appreciated for their ideas and opinions, rewarded for their efforts, and inherently belonging to their society. Accordingly they feel safe and happy most of the time.

The key to understanding the extraordinary power of Dr. Deming's Admonitions is the recognition that they constitute more than a recipe for profitability. Success is more than making money. It involves optimizing as much as possible the quality of life of all involved. For a business it means attending conscientiously to the needs of the company's suppliers, customers, employees, sales force, and advertisers: In short, everyone who comes in contact with the company; and not just the company's owners.

If you think this through, as I have, you recognize that the adoption of Dr. Deming's Admonitions requires a company to become more aware of and more responsive to the personal wishes of all of these people. To accomplish this, a company has to make a moral commitment to a higher standard of ethics than does the company that runs according to hierarchically authoritarian principles. In organizational development terms, the culture of the organization must become ethical. An organization's culture is the model employed to standardize the relationship between a supervisor and a supervisee. We will have more to say about this later.

About the Bill of Ethics
If Dr. Deming's Admonitions can be derived from the *Bill of Ethics* it will prove that the Ethics is at least a logically equivalent statement. In fact we will show that the Ethics is a far more general and far-reaching statement; that Dr. Deming's Admonitions constitute only a small subset of the logical consequences of the Ethics. Moreover, since it is generally agreed that a form of the Admonitions has beneficially transformed Japanese industry, it is a small step inductively to suspect that a similarly committed application of the Ethics might have a vastly greater set of benefits to offer the nation that took the Ethics as seriously as the Japanese took the Admonitions. For this reason it is important to understand the Ethics somewhat before going through the formal steps of the derivation.

Gregory R. Sulliger and I wrote the Ethics as a result of a detailed study that we performed from 1985 to 1992. In this study we analyzed the problems that our species seems to face and looked for plausible solutions to them. Worldwide adoption of the Ethics or its logical equivalent is the only solution we have found so far that appears to be both necessary and sufficient to a thriving humanity. We don't doubt that there are many other possible solutions, but we suspect that most of them will prove to be the logical equivalents of the Ethics. Such logical equivalents are to be highly valued, because individuals who will not take seriously the Ethics in its present form will take some of them seriously.

In 1992, when we set down the Bill of Ethics in its present form, we actually wrote three versions of it: The first is a proposed amendment to the Oregon state constitution; the second is a proposed amendment to the US constitution; and the third is a generic form that can be adopted as an amendment to the constitution or bylaws of any organization. It is this latter form that is included herein.

At that time we had heard of Dr. Deming's work but were unfamiliar with its content. When we started reading the Admonitions we realized that Dr. Deming had caused significant portions of the Ethics to be put into practice on a massive scale in Japan. The success of the Japanese experiment was "proof" of the validity of our work. We put quotes around the word, "proof" in recognition of the fact that the Japanese experiment has not tested all of the logical consequences of the Ethics, only some of them. In fact it has not tested all the consequences of the Admonitions. One cannot know all the logical consequences of any statement with certainty.

What If...
Dr. Deming's Admonitions have been demonstrated to be "true" by the great experiment of the Japanese. I have written this chapter to assert that the Admonitions are part of a greater "truth" that we have described in the Bill of Ethics. There are two parts to this

statement. The first is that the Admonitions are logically contained in the Ethics. The second is to demonstrate the "truth" of the Ethics. The first is just an exercise in logic. The second can only be accomplished by experiment. The point to be made concerning this is that the Japanese experiment demonstrates the "truth" of the portion of the Ethics contained in the Admonitions.

If this seems unclear consider the definition of "true" information. Information is said to be true if belief that it is true increases one's ability to detect, predict, and initiate causal relationships between events in the observable universe. Information is said to be false if belief that it is true limits or reduces one's ability to detect, predict, and initiate causal relationships between such events. If information is neither true nor false it is said to be trivial.

Most valuable information is not true under all circumstances. If the description of those circumstances under which a statement is true are made part of the statement, the truth of that statement becomes very well defined. The statement, "Success will be attained by the company that properly applies the Admonitions", has been proven true for many industrial companies in Japan. Early results from American companies attempting the same experiment indicate that the statement is probably true for American companies as well.

Now consider the statement, "Success will be attained by the company that properly applies the Ethics". If our logic (yet to be stated) is correct, we know this statement to be true within the same limits for which the previous statement is true; because the Admonitions are contained in the Ethics. This fact makes the Ethics very credible.

Based on this line of reasoning we pose the question: What if the statement, "Success will be attained by the organization, government, or species that properly applies the Ethics." is at least equally true? We suspect it is generally true. Our goal is to see the relevant experiments performed. We will return to this line of reasoning in the "So What?" section concluding this article. Meanwhile, just consider: What if..... ?

Restating the Admonitions

Before attempting to derive Dr. Deming's Admonitions we shall first examine them and restate them somewhat without changing their meaning. As described on page 34 of Mary Walton's book they consist of fourteen "points" to be embodied by the successful business, seven "deadly diseases" to be cured and/or avoided, and four "obstacles" to be overcome. As presented they are:

FOURTEEN POINTS:

1. Create constancy of purpose for improvement of product and service.
2. Adopt the new philosophy [the Admonitions]: Mistakes and negativism are unacceptable.
3. Cease dependence on mass inspection.
4. End the practice of awarding business on price tag alone.
5. Improve constantly and forever the system of production and service
6. Institute training. Teach workers to do their jobs.
7. Institute leadership. Help people to do a better job.
8. Drive out fear
9. Break down barriers between staff areas
10. Eliminate slogans, exhortations, and targets for the workforce.
11. Eliminate numerical quotas
12. Remove barriers to pride of workmanship.
13. Institute a vigorous program of education and retraining. Stress teamwork and statistical technique.
14. Take action to accomplish the transformation.

SEVEN DEADLY DISEASES

1. Lack of constancy of purpose.
2. Emphasis on short-term profits.
3. Evaluation by performance, merit rating, or annual review of performance.
4. Mobility of management.
5. Running a company on visible figures alone.

6. Excessive medical costs.
7. Excessive costs of warranty fueled by lawyers that work for contingency fees.

FOUR OBSTACLES [THAT THWART PRODUCTIVITY]
1. Neglect of long range planning.
2. Relying on technology to solve problems.
3. Seeking examples to follow, rather than developing solutions [to problems].
4. Excuses. The belief that, "Our problems are different..."

Now we shall examine and restate these twenty-five Admonitions to make them susceptible to derivation. For starters let's look at Deadly Diseases (6) and (7). We note that these are not features of the company being admonished; nor are they societal features in which any one company can effect change. They are, if anything admonitions to our society at large, not to a company *per se*. A society that properly applied the Ethics might cure these "diseases"; but these two admonitions have no relevance to the individual company; so we delete them from further discussion. Now we have only twenty-three Admonitions with which to deal.

Next we note that Points (1) and (5) say almost the same thing, so we will combine them into one statement about purpose and improvement: "Commit to constantly and forever improve the product, the service, and the system that provides them." This reduces the number of independent statements to twenty-two.

Note that Points (6) and (13) both deal with education. We combine them into the Admonition: "Institute a vigorous program of education, training, and retraining. Teach workers to do their jobs. Stress teamwork and statistical technique". Now there are twenty-one Admonitions with no loss of information.

Finally, we note that there are really only six independent Admonitions, two of which imply the remaining fifteen; as follows:
1. Adopt the new philosophy. Accept the Admonitions.
2. Take action. Accomplish the transformation [implied by the admonitions].

3. Commit to constantly and forever improve the product, the service, and the system that provides them.
4. Institute vigorous education, training, and retraining of workers to do their jobs. Stress teamwork and statistical technique.
5. Institute leadership.
    5.a. Help people do a better job.
    5.b. Encourage pride of workmanship.
    5.c. Provide both opportunity and security, thereby reducing mobility of management.
    5.d. Engage in long range planning.
    5.e. Improve communication and cooperation between staff areas and between people.
6. Do what works; stop doing what doesn't work.
    6.a. Stop mass inspection.
    6.b. Stop basing long range decisions on short term profits.
    6.c. Stop trying to motivate workers with slogans, targets, and exhortations.
    6.d. Stop relying on technology to solve problems.
    6.e. Stop following examples; develop solutions.
    6.f. Stop purchasing based on price tag alone.
    6.g. Drive out fear; stop intimidating your personnel.
        6.g(1) Stop using numerical quotas as "motivation".
        6.g(2) Stop using performance evaluations or reviews.

It is interesting to note that "Institute leadership" (number 5.) is a rather vague admonition. Admonitions (5.a.) through (5.e.) may be seen as a definition of sorts for the word "leadership". Of course we see that if this definition is already known to the company receiving the admonition, then (5.a.) through (5.e.) are redundant. They could be eliminated without loss.

Admonition number (6.) is really a common sense notion. Do what works. Don't do what doesn't work. As strange as it may seem, this is one of the most important of the Admonitions. In hierarchies generally, and in bureaucracies particularly, the decision to knowingly do what does not work is very common; even more so in government and non-profit bureaucracies than in industrial bureaucracies. Still it is common enough in industry to merit special attention.

We define the process of bureaucratization as the systematic destruction of corrective feedback. The noun, "bureaucracy" therefore means an organization of two or more people in which corrective feedback is systematically destroyed. As workers we withhold corrective feedback from our authoritarian "superiors" when we fear the consequences of being heard more than the consequences of remaining silent. Dr. Deming observed that the behaviors listed in (6.a.) through (6.g.) do not work. Given enough time they will destroy the motivation and morale, and hence the effectiveness, of any organization.

Any thoughtful person who has spent more than a day in a bureaucratic work environment knows that the proof of this statement is visible in millions of instances (experiments) each day. The industry of Japan is proof that companies which de-bureaucratize in this sense are vastly more successful than those which don't. Surely these statements conform to our stated definition of "truth".

Do you accept the six revised "points", including the corollaries of point (5.) and point (6.), as a full and adequate statement of Dr. Deming's Admonitions; and agree that they are the logical equivalent of the original twenty-five points; and that they contain no more and no less information than the original twenty-five as applied to an industry? If not please let us hear from you. If so let's move on to a discussion of how the Ethics yields the same information...and more.

The Bill of Ethics Revisited

The Bill of Ethics defines an ethical act as one that increases creativity or any of its logical equivalents for someone without limiting or diminishing these resources for any person. Conversely, an act which limits or diminishes these resources for any person is unethical no matter who benefits from it. The various principles that follow this definition are logical consequences of the definition. In this sense it would be correct to say that all the principles and admonitions that can be derived from the Ethics are derivable from the definition alone.

For the sake of clarity of exposition we will specify the derived principles that lead us to Deming's Admonitions though we understand that while they are collectively sufficient to the derivation they may not all be necessary to it. The resulting redundancy is the result of the commonality of the source from which they derive. In other words the principles derived from the definitions of the Ethics are not entirely independent of one another. We include them all here because they may be necessary to the readers understanding of the derivation, if not to the derivation itself. Accordingly we include six derived principles of the Ethics each of which, with one exception, has a relevant corollary.

They are as follows:

X. Section (1.1.) admonishes us to commit to the pursuit of ethical purposes by ethical means. Its corollary Section (3.01) requires us if so committed to maximize creativity and all of its discernible logical equivalents.

A. Section (3.03) advises us that any act which diminishes or limits another person's creativity is unethical. The corollary (3.06) states that unethical means can never achieve ethical ends.

B. Section (3.07) notes that failure to take ethical action when we are able to do so is unethical. Its corollary (3.08) states that it is unethical to tolerate unethical behavior. Note that this principle derives most easily from Ethic (X.) above. Failure to take ethical action when we are able to do so would violate the commitment to maximize creativity.

C. Section (3.09) tells us that it is ethical to learn for only by doing so can we maximize our own awareness and access to objective truth; both of which are logical equivalents of creativity. The corollary (3.10) is that it is ethical to doubt; for doubt is the seed of which curiosity is the life force and new objective truth is the fruit. Again we see (X.) above leads to the necessity of (C.).

E. Section (4.1) states that the proper (ethical) role of laws, rules, regulations, and (by logical extension) standardized procedures is the empowerment of those persons who have made a moral commitment to live their lives as ethically as they can; who have in effect embraced the Ethics. This section does not have a relevant corollary. While this principle derives directly from the definitions of the Ethics we note that enforcement of any law, rule, or regulation that does not empower creativity must to some degree diminish it. This would violate Ethic (A.) above and would be unethical.

P. Section (4.2) states that it is the further proper (ethical) role of laws, rules, etc. to prohibit unethical behavior by most ethical means possible. Corollary to this Section (4.3) states that it is never the proper role of laws, rules, etc. to intrude, coerce, or interfere in the lives of anyone except as is truly necessary in order to accomplish the aims of Sections (4.1) and (4.2) above...such intrusion even then to be that which is minimally required.

Referring to the above excerpts from the Ethics as Ethic X, Ethic A, Ethic B, Ethic C, Ethic E, and Ethic P we are now ready to actually perform the derivation of Dr. Deming's Admonitions.

The Derivation
Let's start with the first two Admonitions on the revised list. Assume we make the commitment of Ethic X and that we work for a company in which we have the opportunity behave in accordance

with the first two Admonitions. Can we now not adopt the new philosophy? If all the other Admonitions are derivable from the Ethics we have already adopted the new philosophy. On this one let's wait and see. As for admonition (2), which tells us to take action and accomplish the transformation; clearly Ethic B specifically requires us to engage in ethical action whenever we can. Not to do so would be unethical.

Admonition (3) on the revised list tells us to commit to constant and perpetual improvement of the company's product, service, and the system that provides them. This can be seen to be a direct consequence of Ethic X. To see this ask yourself, "How would I recognize an 'improvement' if I saw one. The obvious answer is that someone would have to benefit by it. We recognize a benefit by seeing an increase in creativity or one of its logical equivalents. In other words, Ethic X applied to the workplace requires exactly the same behavioral response as Admonition (3).

Admonition (4) tells us to institute education and training. This admonition can most easily be deduced from Ethic C. It is ethical to learn; therefore it is ethical to teach, educate, and train. If an employer has the means to provide this resource it would be unethical not to (from Ethic B). This makes the tacit assumption that the information being taught is true in the sense that we have discussed.

If Admonition (5), "Institute leadership" has previously been defined by paragraphs (5.a.) through (5.e.), then this admonition is derivable directly from Ethic X. Clearly the terms of paragraphs (5.a.) through (5.e.) are all ethical acts under most circumstances. If "leadership" has not been previously defined in this way we would arrive at the same list of requisite actions in response to Ethic E, which tells us to empower others in their pursuit of ethical goals by ethical means. By examining what it means to "empower" another person we quickly discover that actions (5.a.) through (5.e.) are all necessary conditions for empowerment, though possibly not sufficient in and of themselves.

Objective analysis of American and Japanese industries clearly tells us what works and what doesn't work in industry. Mass inspection, basing of long term decisions on short term profits, motivation by slogan, fixing the system technically without fixing it organizationally, making excuses, purchasing based on price tag alone, failing to develop solutions while copying models, and all forms of motivation by intimidation don't work! To require people to participate in a system that does these things would be unethical and would be prohibited in any company that adopted Ethics A and P. Hence Ethics A and P demand the behavior that results from following Admonition (6.).

Finally we return to the consideration of Admonition (1) We see now that by making the commitment to Ethic X we have in fact "adopted the new philosophy. Hence our derivation is complete and we have shown that Dr. Deming's Admonitions are in fact contained in the **Bill of Ethics**.

QED!

So What?!
As indicated earlier, we define bureaucracy as the systematic elimination, destruction, or avoidance of corrective feedback. In limiting corrective feedback we diminish people's access to objective truth, which is one of the logical equivalents of creativity. So any action, which contributes to the bureaucratization of an organization, is unethical.

Yet bureaucracy is so widespread and pervasive of human culture as to be seen by the public at large as unavoidable, like "death and taxes". In our view bureaucracy is the greatest single cause of evil in the world today. For this reason we applaud Dr. Deming and the legacy of his Admonitions as the greatest innovation in human culture since the "golden rule". We also applaud the Japanese for having had the courage and the wisdom to attempt the application of the Admonitions on a massive scale.

You recall there were two of Dr. Deming's Admonitions that dealt with excessive medical costs and excessive costs of warranty. We dismissed these as not relevant to the domain in which most corporate decisions could have any effect. Within that domain we see that the Admonitions form an ethical foundation adequate for most aspects of business. Why then do we imply that there is an advantage to be gained by replacing the Admonitions with the Ethics? If the leaders of a business cannot effect change in medical costs and costs or warranty, who can?

Obviously we are addressing the needs of a bigger system here than those of a single business, or even the concatenation of all businesses. There are many organizations to which the Admonitions could not easily be applied; yet to which the Ethics might easily be adapted.

Unions, political parties, clerical groups, charities, research institutions, schools and universities comprise a few groups that are heavily bureaucratized and which would benefit enormously by being de-bureaucratized via the Ethics. Even more in need of such de-bureaucratization are governments and their departments, agencies, bureaus, legislatures, executives, cabinets, and minions in all their various forms. And finally, the most difficult undertaking, the military establishment and its traditionally entrenched hierarchic structures might conceivably be de-bureaucratized one day.

A world in which most of these transitions has been achieved would be almost unrecognizable by today's standards; almost inconceivable. Yet we ask ourselves, "If not in this way, how; if not now, when will peace and opportunity become universally available?"

APPENDIX G: FURTHER READING AND STUDY

- **BORG WARS,** by Robert Podolsky
  This little book provides a detailed explanation of the BIG PROBLEM, its origins, and manifestations.

- **MAKE IT SO!,** by Robert Podolsky:
  More about Titania and the proposed solution to the BIG PROBLEM, with examples and practical applications.

- **HEART AND MIND,** by Robert Podolsky:
  Poems, fables, and metaphors for your Right Brain and some more detailed intellectual analyses for your Left Brain.

- **The BORG MATRIX,** by Robert Podolsky:
  BORG WARS for high school and college kids.

- **CREATIVE TRANSFORMATION,** by John David Garcia: covers the evolution of matter, the evolution of life, the evolution of awareness, the evolution of consciousness, the evolution of evolution, and many topics relevant to understanding creativity, ethics, and applications to social organization. Very advanced, with no concessions to vocabulary or complexity, this book is excellent – but not for the intellectually challenged.

- **COMMON SENSE REVISITED**, by Clyde Cleveland.

- **RESTORING THE HEART OF AMERICA**, by Clyde Cleveland

- **They Own It All – Including You,** by Ronald McDonald

- **BIRTH of the CHAORDIC AGE**
  by Dee Hock

- **LAUNCHING A LEADERSHIP REVOLUTION,**
  by Chris Brady and Orrin Woodward.

- **Resolved,** by Chris Brady and Orrin Woodward.

- **Leadership and Liberty,** by Chris Brady and Orrin Woodward.

- **Leadershift**, *by* Orrin Woodward

- **Out of the Crisis,** by William Deming

- **TITANIAN WEBSITE:**
  https://www.titanians.org

Business and Money

Aguano, Rafael: *Dr. Deming*, Simon & Schuster, 1990

Blanchard, Kenneth & Johnson, Spencer: *The One-Minute Manager*, Berkley Books, 1981

Browne, Harry. How I Found Freedom in an Unfree World. Avon, 1973.

Fisher, Roger & Ury, William: *Getting to Yes*, Houghton Mifflin, 1983

Frost, Ted S.: *Where Have all the Woolly Mammoths Gone?*, Parker Publishing, 1976

Gerber, Michael: *The E-Myth Revisited*, Harper Collins, 1995

Griffin, G. Edward: *The Creature from Jekyll Island (Audio Tape or CD),* American Media, 1998.

Hopkins, Tom: *How to Master the Art of Selling,* Warner Books, 1980

Kiyosaki, Robert: *Rich Dad, Poor Dad, The Cashflow Quadrant,* and *Rich Dad's Guide to Investing.*

Phillips, Michael: *The Seven Laws of Money*, Word Wheel and Random House, 1974.

Walton, Mary: *The Deming Management Method*, Putnam Publishing, 1986

Ethics

Garcia, John David: *Creative Transformation,* Noetic Press and Whitmore Publishing Co. Inc., 1991

Machan, Tibor. Capitalism and Individualism. St. Martin's Press, 1990.

Machan, Tibor. Commerce and Morality. Rowman & Littlefield, 1988.

Rothbard, Murray: *For a New Liberty*, Macmillan Press, 1973

Sowell, Thomas. The Quest for Cosmic Justice. The Free Press, 1999.

Fiction

Donaldson, Stephen: *The Chronicles of Thomas Covenant* (double trilogy)

Rand, Ayn. Atlas Shrugged. New American Library, 1957.

Rand, Ayn. The Fountainhead. Bobbs-Merrill, 1943.

Tolkien, J.R.R.: *The Hobbit,* and *Lord of the Rings (trilogy)*

Madwoman of Chaillot, The

Moon and Sixpence, The

Government

Bandow, Doug. The Politics of Plunder. Transaction Publishers, 1990.

Bovard, James. Freedom in Chains: The Rise of the State and the Demise of the Citizen. Palgrave Macmillan, 2000.

Bovard, James. Lost Rights: The Destruction of American Liberty. St. Martin's Press, 1995.

Boaz, David. Libertarianism: A Primer. The Free Press, 1997.

Browne, Harry. Why Government Doesn't Work. St. Martin's Press, 1995.

Bartlett, Donald & Steele, James: *America: What Went Wrong*, Andrews and McMeel, 1992.

Flew, Antony. Equality in Liberty and Justice. Transaction Publishers, 2001.

Friedman, Milton and Rose. Free to Choose. Harcourt Brace Jovanovich, 1979.

Friedman, Milton. Capitalism and Freedom. University of Chicago Press, 1962.

Hayek, F.A. Law, Legislation and Liberty, Vol. 3, The Political Order of a Free People. University of Chicago, 1979.

Hayek, F.A. Law, Legislation and Liberty, Vol. 2, The Mirage of Social Justice. University of Chicago Press, 1976.

Hayek, F.A. Law, Legislation and Liberty, Vol. 1, Rules and Order. University of Chicago Press, 1973.

Hayek, F.A. The Constitution of Liberty. University of Chicago Press, 1960.

Hayek, F.A. The Road to Serfdom. University of Chicago Press, 1944.

Hazlitt, Henry. Economics in One Lesson. Three Rivers Press, 1988.

Hightower, Jim: *There's Nothing in the Middle of the Road but Yellow Stripes and Dead Armadillos,*

Hoppe, Hans-Hermann. Democracy: The God That Failed. Transaction Publishers, 2001.

Hospers, John. Libertarianism: A Political Philosophy for Tomorrow. Nash Publishing, 1971.

Liddy, G. Gordon. When I was a Kid, This Was a Free Country. Regnery, 2002.

Marshall, Will and Schram, Martin: *Mandate for Change*, Berkley Books, 1993.

Mises, Ludwig von. The Anti-Capitalistic Mentality. D. Van Nostrand Company, 1956.

Nozick, Robert. Anarchy, State and Utopia. Basic Books, 1974.

Osborne, David & Gaebler, Ted: *Reinventing Government*, Penguin Books, 1992.

Sheeran, Michael: *Beyond Majority Rule*, Religious Society of Friends, 1983

Rand, Ayn. Capitalism: The Unknown Ideal. New American Library, 1986.

Rothbard, Murray. N. Man, Economy and State. The Mises Institute, 2004.

Rothbard, Murray N. The Ethics of Liberty. New York University Press, 1998.

Rothbard, Murray. N. For a New Liberty. Libertarian Review Foundation, 1978.

Life & Personal Evolution

Grinder, John & Bandler, Richard: *Frogs Into Princes*, Real People Press, 1979 and *The Structure of Magic*, and *The Structure of Magic II,* Science & Behavior Books, 1975 and 1976.

Lao Tsu (as translated by Gia-Fu Feng and Jane English): *Tao Te Ching*.

Taylor, Jim and Wacker, Watts: *The 500-Year Delta*, Harper Collins, 1997.

Toffler, Alvin: *Future Shock* and *The Third Wave*, Mass Market Paperbacks, 1970 and 1980 respectively

WORTHWHILE LINKS

http://www.famguardian.org

http://goldmoney.com/

http://jcc.sagepub.com/cgi/content/refs/35/1/29

http://news.bbc.co.uk/1/hi/world/americas/4430491.stm

http://nightweed.com/usavotefacts.html

http://realityzone.com/

http://triallogs.blogspot.com/

http://turbulence.org/Works/swipe/main.html

http://www.861.info/tessa.html

http://www.911inplanesite.com/

http://www.aclu.org/freedomwire/

http://www.adl.org/

http://www.amazon.com/gp/product/061512321X/002-02161046317624?v=glance&n=283155&n=507846&s=books&v=glance

http://www.amazon.com/gp/product/096404479X/002-0216104-6317624?v=glance&n=283155

http://www.americanlawrview.com/2nd_amend.html

http://www.copwatch.org/reforms.html

http://www.freedom-force.org/

http://www.freemarketnews.com/

http://www.freestarmedia.com/hotellostliberty1.html

http://www.gemworld.com/usavsus.htm

http://www.geocities.com/northstarzone/index.html

http://www.geoffmetcalf.com/790.html

http://www.givemeliberty.org/

http://www.givemeliberty.org/RTPLawsuit/Update2005-05-21.htm

http://www.globalresearch.ca/index.php?context=viewArtcle&code=WHI20051113&articleId=1240

http://www.gunowners.org/

http://www.harrybrowne.org/

http://www.harrybrowne.org/TopicalIndex.htm#p

http://www.hawaii.edu/powerkills/LIST.HTM

http://www.ij.org/

http://www.infowars.com/

http://www.lewrockwell.com/

http://www.lewrockwell.com/orig3/victor3.html

http://www.lewrockwell.com/orig3/victor4.html

http://www.lonsberry.com/writings.cfm?story=1687

http://www.michnews.com/cgi-bin/artman/exec/view.cgi/145/7968

http://www.mmbfavorites.blogspot.com/

http://www.newstarget.com/012923.html

http://www.ninehundred.net/banister/Exhibit%205%20Report%20Transmittal.pdf

http://www.ninehundred.net/banister/Exhibit%207%20Varville%20Memorandum.pdf

http://www.paynoincometax.com/

http://www.quotegarden.com/election-day.html

http://www.theft-by-deception.com/

http://www.titanians.org/

http://www.worldnetdaily.com/

Alphabetical Index

Amendment..159p., 191

American Medical Association................................49

Amin...50

Anarchy...207

Authors' Experience, The.......................................59

Bandow, Doug..205

Beliefs and belief systems.....49p., 61, 80, 165, 168p.

    Faith..48

Bill of Ethics....................154, 188, 190p., 196, 200

Bill of Rights..63

Blanchard, Kenneth...203

Bloodless Revolution..63p.

Boaz, David..205

BORG..50

Bovard, James...205

Browne, Harry..203, 205

Bureaucracy...........................62, 174, 196, 200

Business...........62, 106, 172, 188, 190, 193, 201, 203

Caesar..50

Child...189

Commerce...189

Creative Transformation...............................154

Creativity..173

Creature from Jekyll Island, The...................204

Crime..63

Definitions...169

Deming, William E......................................203p.

Deming, Wm. Edward........187pp., 193, 196pp., 200p.

Democratic Fallacy....................................49, 206

Distrust...157

Doc Oyanitu.........................106, 108pp., 113

Dr. Deming's \..193

Dr. Deming's Fourteen Points......................193

Education......................................193pp., 199

Ethic..................................154pp., 190, 196pp.

Ethical Means and Ethical Ends...................165

    Golden Rule Proof......................................174

    Historical Proof...168

Logical Proof...175

Types of "Sins..165

Ethics..168, 170pp., 204, 207

Evolution..155p., 207

Exploitation...63, 168

Fear...189, 193, 195p.

Flew, Antony...205

Friedman, Milton..205p.

Genghis Kahn..50

Genocide..50, 168

God...60, 206

Government....48p., 63, 167p., 171p., 188, 192, 196, 201, 205, 207

   Leaders..193, 195, 199

   Communist..49

Greed..190

Greetings from Titania.......................................106

Gregory R. Sulliger..153

Harm..158p.

Hayek, F.A..206

Hazlitt, Henry..206

Hitler..50

Hoppe, Hans-Herman..206

Hospers, John...206

Ignorance..165

Incompetence...159

Institutions.............................61, 168, 172p., 176

Intelligence...169

Isms..

    Nationalism..61

    Racism..61

    Religionism..61

    Sexism..61

Japanese...187pp., 200

Jim Hightower...206

John David Garcia...........................154, 174, 204

Johnson, Spencer...203

Karl Marx...172

Law..157

Legend of Odoka, The....................................102pp.

Liberals..82

Libertarianism...207

Liddy, G. Gordon..206

Louis Pasteur...49

Machan, Tibor..204

Marshall, Will...206

McCarthy Era...49

Meaning..193

Means...157

Media...204pp.

Midéwiwin...59

Mises, Ludwig von..207

Model..190, 200

Money...190

Napoleon Hill..64

Nozick, Robert...207

Peace...60p., 168, 175, 201

Peron..50

Person.........................154pp., 158p., 190, 195pp.

Politics..205p.

Poverty	62, 168, 171
Profit	190, 193, 195p., 200
Rand, Ayn	205, 207
Religion	171
Catholic	48
Christian	48
Muslim	49
Robin Hood Fallacy	49
Schram, Martin	206
Slavery	62, 168, 171
Soviet Union	48, 174
Sowell, Thomas	204
Spaceship Earth	61
Stalin	50
Statistical quality control	187
Syzygy	108p., 111pp.
Taxes	200
Ten Suggestions	146
THE BILL OF ETHICS	154
COOPERATION OF OFFICIALS	159

DEFINITIONS..155

INTRODUCTION..154

LAWS, RULES AND REGULATIONS......................158

PHILOSOPHY & RATIONALE................................154

PREAMBLE..154

PREVIOUSLY EXISTING RULES AND POLICIES......159

PRINCIPLES..156

Titania...

   Citizen...205

Truth and Falsehood...................49p., 64, 168pp., 173

Tyranny of the Majority..49

United States...................................49, 62, 173p.

Values and beliefs...168

Walton, Mary...204

War........................49, 61, 155pp., 172, 188p., 193p.

THE TITANIA HOLOMAT

The diagram to the left represents a future stage in the development of the **Titania HoloMat**. As shown, it is comprised of 13 smaller HoloMats of 8 Octologues each – where each Octologue is represented by a small purple octagon. At this stage the population of the HoloMat will be about 576.

Note too that the organization is divided according to functional units for purposes of coordinating the many interrelated activities that its operation will require.

As you read this, the authors are already recruiting members and commencing the training activities that the methodology demands. Projects offering paid positions will soon be coming on line. If you have skills that might be helpful to this HoloMat, please contact cronus@titanians.org for more information.

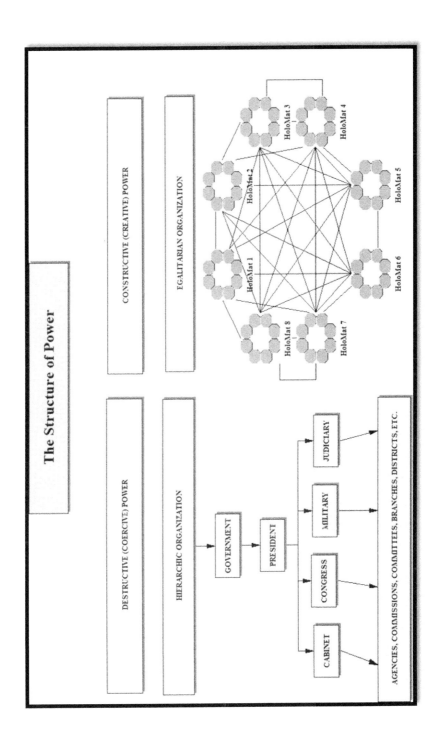

Printed in Great Britain
by Amazon